dailylove

D1331879

daily love

GROWING *into* GRACE

Mastin Kipp

HAY HOUSE

Carlsbad, California • New York City • London • Sydney
Johannesburg • Vancouver • Hong Kong • New Delhi

First published and distributed in the United Kingdom by:
Hay House UK Ltd, Astley House, 33 Notting Hill Gate, London W11 3JQ
Tel: +44 (0)20 3675 2450; Fax: +44 (0)20 3675 2451
www.hayhouse.co.uk

Published and distributed in the United States of America by:
Hay House Inc., PO Box 5100, Carlsbad, CA 92018-5100
Tel: (1) 760 431 7695 or (800) 654 5126
Fax: (1) 760 431 6948 or (800) 650 5115
www.hayhouse.com

Published and distributed in Australia by:
Hay House Australia Ltd, 18/36 Ralph St, Alexandria NSW 2015
Tel: (61) 2 9669 4299; Fax: (61) 2 9669 4144
www.hayhouse.com.au

Published and distributed in the Republic of South Africa by:
Hay House SA (Pty) Ltd, PO Box 990, Witkoppen 2068
Tel/Fax: (27) 11 467 8904
www.hayhouse.co.za

Published and distributed in India by:
Hay House Publishers India, Muskaan Complex, Plot No.3, B-2,
Vasant Kunj, New Delhi 110 070
Tel: (91) 11 4176 1620; Fax: (91) 11 4176 1630
www.hayhouse.co.in

Distributed in Canada by:
Raincoast Books, 2440 Viking Way, Richmond, B.C. V6V 1N2
Tel: (1) 604 448 7100; Fax: (1) 604 270 7161; www.raincoast.com

Copyright © 2014 by Daily Love Media, Inc.

The moral rights of the author have been asserted.

Front-cover and interior design: Celia Fuller-Vels

"Mighty to Save" Copyright © 2006 Hillsong Music Publishing (APRA)
(adm. in the US and Canada at CapitolCMGPublishing.com).
All rights reserved. Used by permission.

All rights reserved. No part of this book may be reproduced by any mechanical,
photographic or electronic process, or in the form of a phonographic recording;
nor may it be stored in a retrieval system, transmitted or otherwise be copied
for public or private use, other than for 'fair use' as brief quotations embodied
in articles and reviews, without prior written permission of the publisher.

The information given in this book should not be treated as a substitute for
professional medical advice; always consult a medical practitioner. Any use
of information in this book is at the reader's discretion and risk. Neither the
author nor the publisher can be held responsible for any loss, claim or damage arising out of the use, or misuse, of the suggestions made, the failure to
take medical advice or for any material on third party websites.

A catalogue record for this book is available from the British Library.

ISBN: 978-1-78180-103-1

Printed and bound in Great Britain by TJ International, Padstow, Cornwall.

To Mom, Dad, Jenna,
Dolly, Alan, and Sadie.
Thank you for being a
powerful example of
Love in my life.
I owe it all to you.

ABERDEENSHIRE LIBRARIES	
3152114	
Bertrams	03/11/2014
362.29	£10.99

CONTENTS

FOREWORD

M<small>Y WIFE AND I LIVE IN A HOME IN</small> V<small>ENICE</small>, CA, <small>WHICH IS</small> lovingly dubbed "The Appleton Ashram." It is spacious, with a temple-like energy, lots of light, wood floors, and a large garden out back. People visit often. Some will stay for tea or a green juice or a smoothie. Others come to practice meditation or yoga or to partake in a 12-Step meeting. People come and people go. One day, Mastin just came.

There is a very comfortable green couch in our living room, which would become Mastin's bed for several months in early 2010. We would have a chance to get to know each other and develop a close friendship during that time. It was a great blessing for both of us.

Mastin made it clear up front that he was in a difficult spot in life, that there was great uncertainty. He had this unusual ability to explain clearly what the issues were and a truly sweet willingness to turn his gaze within. He was in a real crisis, but refused to look away. Mastin had the desire to speak about it and to go through the actual feeling of his suffering.

Even more remarkable, however, was the depth of Mastin's honesty. Unlike anyone I had known, Mastin had developed a keen ability to tell the truth as he saw it. Frankly, it was disarming. As trust grew between us, he exercised greater and greater license to speak his innermost truths, making himself completely vulnerable. There were a few times that Mastin put voice to some of his shadows and my reaction was to simply laugh, only because one doesn't often get to hear someone be that honest. Of course by doing so, Mastin was inadvertently empowering me to look at and express my own shadows. Such is the power of the book before you.

While all of this was going on, Mastin was performing a daily spiritual practice, which yogis refer to as *sadhana*. The yogis believe that one's commitment to their sadhana is an indicator of strength and devotion. Mastin's sadhana was The Daily Love. Every day without fail he would disappear and tend to the sacred contract he had with his Higher Power and the rather huge community of people who had come to read The Daily Love. There were a few times when he would grumble about it. I'm ashamed to admit this, but there were even a few times I would try to get him to blow it off so we could hang out—but he never missed it. His devotion to The Daily Love was unwavering.

I can attest to Mastin's utter fascination and scholarship when it comes to words, teachings, and teachers. These have been the currency of our collective transformation as members of The Daily Love community. If you want to know when Mastin is happiest (except when he's hanging out with his girlfriend, Jenna) just watch him have a discourse with a teacher such as Tony Robbins or Caroline Myss or any other who authentically assists people in the move toward truth. You would note that Mastin demonstrates what is perhaps the rarest of assets in our world today: Mastin listens. He may not always agree with the opinions or ideas he is taking in, but I have sat back and watched in wonder at his ability to consider information, absorb what is meaningful to him, and integrate it into immediately applicable lessons. And I've seen him apply those lessons, skillfully crafting language on the spot to uplift a person out of the depths of despair, give them a sense of hope, and provide them with actual action steps to move ahead.

As Mastin's brother on the path, I was super-honored that he asked me to write the foreword to his book. And I have been meticulous in reading it. I'm watching out for one thing only—Mastin's authentic voice and truth. Nothing affects me as much as the truth laid out in someone's authentic voice. Well, Mastin has laid it out for you in the plainest, most honest and raw terms. Part of his strength and effectiveness as a teacher is that he sees himself as a work in progress. With *Daily Love*, he is absolutely committed to getting you the truth, the whole truth and nothing but the truth. And it will come in his vernacular. He proclaims himself a geek, drug addict, and college dropout. He waxes philosophic about *Star Wars* and *Star Trek*. He speaks openly about the many ass-whoopings that he's taken, and for this I love him even more. What thrills me most about this book is the way Mastin has laid out his psychological, emotional, and spiritual processes as his life unfolded into the light of Grace. *Daily*

Love is the real thing. This is what actually happened, inside and out. I can vouch for its authentic voice because I was there on the green couch for many a late-night session.

It takes a brave person to truly drop their armor and allow you to see within. There is freedom in the truth. It does set you free. With *Daily Love*, Mastin lays it out for your consideration. And he will not skip the parts that most of us would prefer to leave out of our own tale. He will tell you of his driving need for significance and the prices he has had to pay for that. He will also tell you of his driving need to contribute to humanity and his yearning for the day "when the importance of compassion and Love are self-evident."

This is a hopeful book. It will make you smile and cry and fill you with inspiration. It is the true story of an underdog who grew to see his dreams come true and who continues to dream into the reaches of the unknown as a way of life. It is an all-access pass to bare witness to a man's intimate, moving, and magical journey through his dark night of the soul. Where once Mastin may have written this book out of a need for significance, my impression in reading it is that this is his continuing contribution to humanity and his personal request that we hear "the whisper that lay within us" and commit to following our dreams. This is Mastin's invitation to us all to drop our armor, to be free, and to "Be Love."

Tommy Rosen
Venice, CA 2014

INVOCATION

A DAY WILL COME WHEN YOU WILL BE STIRRED BY UNEX-
pected events. A part of you will die and you will begin to
search for the elixir to bring this part of you back to life. You
will seek this elixir in friends, lovers, enemies, books, religions, foreign countries, heroes, songs, rituals, and jobs. But
no matter where you look, the treasure will evade you.

All will seem lost. You will lose all hope that this magic
potion even exists. It will be the darkest of nights, and the
promise of certain death will lead you to the abyss of despair.
But, staring into this abyss, you will begin to see the dim light
of your own illumined soul.

Your radiance will transform the abyss itself into the elu-
sive elixir of life. And for the first time you will realize that
all the while . . . it was your own Light that you were searching
for.

— chapter 1 —

THANK YOU FOR YOUR ATTENTION

Everything that needs to be said has already been said. But since no one was listening, everything must be said again.

—ANDRÉ GIDE

I THINK DEEP DOWN, WE'RE ALL LOOKING FOR GRACE. IT'S what we feel when we fall in love, look into a child's eyes, or watch the sunset over the Pacific on a perfect LA night. It's also the feeling most of us are looking for when we get involved in something that's loosely termed "spirituality." The concept of spirituality has never been more popular than it is today, understandably, considering our environmental, economic, and religious troubles. With a world arguably teetering on the brink of disaster, it's no surprise we would be seeking "personal growth" and spirituality. It's a way each of us can make a difference, starting with ourselves.

It's possible that you've read my blog, *The Daily Love*, and we've inspired you—and/or annoyed you at times—with our daily e-mails. Or maybe you have no idea who the heck I am, and a friend pushed this book on you in hopes it might help you take the next step on your journey. Or, maybe it just fell off the shelf and hit you in the head (please sue the bookstore, not me) and you decided to read it. Either way, welcome to my crazy world.

Since *The Daily Love* started on social media, and the average time people spend on my site is about five minutes, I do not take your attention for granted.

I'm grateful for it.

My guess is that you've been guided to this book for some reason or other. Maybe you feel stuck. Maybe you've bottomed out. Or perhaps you really want to transform your life. Whatever brought us together for the next little while, I'm choosing to believe we've been guided to meet—that we're here to help each other.

In the next couple hundred pages or so I'll be sharing my often fun, almost lethal, and sometimes comical story. Hopefully it will inspire you to take even more risks than you have up until this point. Hopefully we'll laugh together, cry together, and perhaps even have a few "aha" moments together.

don't be impressed

I have the honor of being in the in-boxes of hundreds of thousands of people each day. We've had millions of people come to our website, and I've sold out retreats, seminars, and events all over the globe, from Maui to Bali, from Australia to Europe to Jamaica and all over the United States. I've also been featured as a "new generation spiritual thinker" by Oprah Winfrey on her weekly show, *Super Soul Sunday*.

Please do not let any of this impress you. If you only knew me! Like you, perhaps, I'm messed up, imperfect, and *really* good at making mistakes. I've been addicted to drugs. I've broken hearts. I've lied. I'm a recovering Christian and recovering Love Addict. I've been an asshole. I've held on to grievances a lot longer than I should have. I've gambled away college money. I've stolen money from my parents. I'm a college dropout. As of the writing of this book, the only formal training I've completed is as a yoga teacher. Okay?

Still want to listen to me? If not, I would understand. Hey, you might even still have time to return this book!

So I don't have a fancy degree to hang on my wall and show you. I don't come with all the bells and whistles. I'm rough around the edges. But what I do have is life, and scars. I have experience. I've overcome broken hearts and licked the self-inflicted wounds of my own ego. I've recovered from cocaine and Adderall addictions.

I've also built a community where you will always be welcome—a place where you can feel like you belong. That place is called *The Daily Love*. For reasons I may never understand, millions of people seem to trust what I have to say. They, like you, come looking for a sense of community on their journey—and they find it on our site.

Now that said, please do not take everything I share in this book as gospel. It's not "the" Truth. There is no such thing as "the" Truth—there is just what you believe to be true, and what I believe to be true. And perhaps we share some of those beliefs. I'm open to my beliefs changing, and I hope, for your sake, that you are open to your beliefs changing, too. I have a fierce belief in what's possible for you, and I have unwavering certainty that for you, dear Seeker, the best is yet to come. Please take what resonates with you in this book and leave the rest.

just a kid from Kansas

Long before millions of people came to my website, I was just a kid from Kansas. I wasn't even supposed to be born. If my mother had listened to her doctors, I wouldn't exist. (More on that later.) I'm a product of public school and big dreams. I've been rejected by a lot of women. Like, *a lot*. (More on that later, too.) And I'm a geek. There was a time in my life when I literally would have chosen computer games over true love.

But I've also tried my best to make the world a better place before I die. My father said if I could do that, I'd have lived a good life.

I've always been curious about why people do what they do and how to make the human condition better. My methods for discovering these things may be off the beaten path, but I've come to some kind of peace about being outside the mainstream. Deep down I know we're more the same than we are different.

So, why should you listen to the college dropout former addict computer geek? Well, truth is I've come a long way. I've been down many of the paths that await you. Think of me as a well-journeyed traveler who can help guide you through the uncertainty that lies ahead. I can tell you where the cliffs are slippery and the sun burns hot. I can help you learn to trust yourself and turn any trauma into power.

Why can I do this? Because I've walked the path myself. It's a path I like to call the journey from crisis to Grace. Don't get me wrong—I'm still being forged in the fire. I'm not finished yet. You see, to be human is to be in crisis. From the moment we are born, we are in crisis (i.e., we're in a situation that we can't control). It's called life. But the good news is that within life there are certain cycles, or patterns, that you can learn to recognize. This book is about one of those patterns. My hope is that by the time you finish reading it, you'll be able to recognize and maneuver this pattern a little bit more easily.

Just being human is a crisis of sorts. We're pushed out of a quiet, warm, safe womb into the cold, loud, unprotected world—and so the catastrophe begins. For most of us, a measure of pain and suffering ensues, following us around for the next 60 or 80 years. And yet at the same time, this crisis is an opportunity. For if we can figure out how to relax, find our power, and learn from our difficulties, we can turn this out-of-control situation called life into something truly wonder-full.

In other words, wonder is possible in every moment—if we allow Grace to enter. For Grace arrives the moment we decide to let go of what we can't control, focus on what we can control, and let Something Greater take over.

grace vs. "spirituality"

Spirituality is the measure of how Loving a person can be. It's the measure of how willing we are to allow Grace—some power greater than ourselves—to enter our lives and guide us along our way. But that's just me. Get a room full of a thousand people and ask each one of them what spirituality means to them, and the definition will start to get blurry. It isn't the same as asking someone to define a word like *car* or *sun*. Any consensus you might get will be vague at best. And with vagueness comes confusion.

One thing I love is clarity. I like to know what the heck things mean. So many people today are throwing around words and phrases like *spirituality, intention, highest potential, higher self, purpose, attraction, vibration*. The list goes on and on. We can form pretty sentences like, "My intention is to raise my vibration to the level of my highest self so I can reach the goal of my highest potential and FINALLY live my purpose and attract an amazing life!" It sounds good, doesn't it? But what does it *mean*? Did the person who said this know what he or she was talking about? To me, undefined spiritual lingo is poetry at best—manipulation and control at worst.

And what it often leaves out, in my humble opinion, is room for Grace. The uncontrollable, benevolent, Loving power of the Divine that wants to enter the world through and as YOU. So why aren't all of us living in the middle of that kind of Grace? For many of us in the so-called spiritual world, it's because there's no room! We're so stuffed up with ideas about what is spiritual (chanting om, biking to work, eating raw food) and what is not (TV, junk food, plastic bottles) that we haven't left room for it. The good news is that even if most of us don't consciously leave room for Grace, Grace will find a way. Whether we like it or not, and using whatever tools are necessary. Even if that means shaking our foundations so strongly we lose all sense of control and don't know which way is up. Yep, it sometimes takes nothing less than a life-shattering crisis to break up the soil and let Grace unfurl.

That's what this book is about: the cycle of crisis to Grace. But what I've learned, by going through this cycle over and over (and over—as you'll soon see), is that there *is* something to this whole "spirituality" thing. I've learned that spirituality does not avert crisis—crisis is a part of the human condition. But what spirituality *does* do is help us better navigate our lives so that the cycle of crisis to Grace isn't as bumpy. When we behave in ways that are truly spiritual, there are fewer struggles and less suffering. We can ride the waves of crisis with more surrender, and in that way we allow Grace to carry us.

my core assumptions about spirituality

Spirituality may be difficult to define (try looking it up in *Webster's* and making any sense of what you find there) and it may be misused and misunderstood, but I believe in spirituality. To me, being spiritual means living a life where there's room for Grace to enter. So before we start on the journey of this book together, let's make sure you and I are on the same page. Let me explain a few core assumptions I make—basically, what spirituality means to me.

I start with a core assumption about the Divine. I believe that a Higher Power, or Source, created and sustains all matter. In my blog at TheDailyLove.com, I call this Higher Power the "Uni-verse." I punctuate it in an unconventional way because I want to emphasize the roots of the word *uni-verse*. The first part, *uni*, means "one." The second part, *verse*, means "song." This makes perfect sense to me. We are all here together, singing one song. We came from, and will return to, the same place. I see the Uni-verse as a term that is designed to unite, rather than divide. There's enough division in this world already—enough suffering and pain due to difference and disconnection. My aim is to focus on what we have in common and hopefully bring more peace to the planet. So for the sake of this book, I am going to say that the Uni-verse is a Higher Power that created all of Life, and we come from it and return to it.

I will use words and phrases like *God*, *the Uni-verse*, *the Divine*, and *Source* throughout this book. To me, they all mean the same thing.

The second core assumption I'm making is that energy cannot be created or destroyed; it simply changes forms. This is true in physics, and as I see it, it's true in the metaphysical universe as well. From this assumption, we can extrapolate that we do not die—we simply change forms.

My third core assumption is actually more of a definition. A definition of a term I use a lot: Love. While there are many ways to talk about Love, I think it all boils down to one thing. To me, "Love" means unconditional acceptance of "what is." It means not rejecting, trying to change, manipulating, or ignoring the truth of what's happening right now. Instead, it's being willing to stay with whatever is, regardless of whether it's pleasurable or painful.

My last core assumption is that I believe each of our lives has a purpose that was planted within us by the Uni-verse. I call this purpose our "Gift." You were born with something that only you can give to the world, and if you don't give it, the world will be less. Finding out what your purpose, your gift, is and giving it to the world is the most important thing you can do in your lifetime.

I'm glad that you understand my core assumptions because each one has a role to play within my definition of "being spiritual." From my perspective, being spiritual means *unconditionally accepting what is, while expressing the gift that God gave each of us in the world.*

More simply, being spiritual means Being Love, while giving your gift to the world.

the measure of what's spiritual

Spirituality isn't about being gluten-free, wearing Lululemon, doing vinyasas, chanting mantras, going to church, tithing, doing self-help seminars, being vegan, being vegetarian, reading self-help books, subscribing to *The Daily Love* or any other *thing* that you *do*. While all these choices are awesome, in my estimation, they don't equate with being spiritual. You can wear all the right clothes and spend your days at an ashram and still act like a jerk. At its essence, spirituality is a measure of how Loving you are, how unconditionally accepting you are toward yourself and others.

To me, spirituality is a living practice. You don't need to go to Italy, India, or Bali to find your spirituality, although those places may be lovely to visit. It's right here in front of you right now. It's in every person you meet and every breath you take. It's everywhere you go, though you can't see it. You certainly can't buy it. And you won't find it in a book.

I know what you're thinking: *WTF? Why did I go buy this book, then? I wonder what the return policy is.* If you'll just hold off for a minute, I'll attempt to explain myself out of the hole I just dug.

My point is that none of these "things" matter if you aren't being Loving.

The external markers I mentioned above are potential *gateways* to learning how to Love, but they are not the Loving itself, because Love itself can only be found within you. That's the promise and that's the bitch. You think you need to go to all these exotic places to find it, but it's not out there—it's in *here*!

But where *in here?* you might wonder. *My mind? My heart? My lungs? My feet? My toes? My ankles? My eyebrows? Where is this spirituality thing? WHERE IS THE LOVE INSIDE OF ME?*

Here comes one of the most important lessons I ever learned.

The Love is in the choices we make.

Period.

Being Love is a living thing, a moment-by-moment practice. If you're anything like me, you'll be refining it and trying to get it right for the rest of your life. And good for you, because people who are trying to be Loving are my kind of people. I'd rather hang out with a Loving member of an opposing political party, or a Loving carnivore atheist, than I would a cold-hearted yogi, no matter how long they've been a gluten-free vegan or how many times they've chanted at the altar of Shiva.

I've learned that when we begin to understand what spirituality is—and we begin to shift our lives toward unconditional Love—we start to see ourselves differently. We see that everyone has a gift to give to the world. All of us are both teachers and students. We are givers and receivers. We are unique and to be celebrated. When we go one step deeper, we start to see that we are the Divine's gift to the world. All of us. Including me. Even though, as you'll see, my journey has been pretty messy.

What follows is a story that sometimes makes me proud, but more often makes me cringe. I have made a lot of mistakes. I've held God at arm's length. I've tried to control my circumstances to get what I wanted and ended up falling flat on my face. But there, in my darkest hour, I've also been saved. I've been helped back to my feet by innumerable teachers and friends. I've gotten the right message at precisely the right moment. And I've been redeemed by Love—my own, and the Love that's poured in from the Uni-verse when I least expected it and least deserved it.

So in hopes it may help you, inspire you, or just make you feel less alone, I am grateful for the chance to share with you my story—a story of the journey from crisis to Grace.

— chapter 2 —

A SOLID FOUNDATION

*If I have seen further it is by standing
on the shoulders of giants.*

—ISAAC NEWTON

THERE'S NO SUCH THING AS A SELF-MADE HUMAN BEING. We've all had help—moments of pure Grace that go beyond what our own self-will can do. Hard work is important, of course, but to say that any of us is self-made is inaccurate.

We are able to shine because of those who have come before us, and those who have Loved and supported us before we could Love and support ourselves. Like many who have come to the point in their lives where they have written a book—a book they believe can add some kind of value to the world—I did not start out wise. I feel like my soul decided to learn patience in this lifetime, because none of the lessons have come fast for me. I've spent more time than I'd like to admit being rude, arrogant, self-righteous, impatient, and stressed-out. I've been an overeater, a bulimic, and a drug addict. The road of my life is paved in mistakes, mishaps, and all kinds of good intentions gone wrong.

My friend Tommy often shares a story about "enlighten-ment" that makes me feel a little better about how my life has gone: A student asks his teacher how to attain enlight-enment. The teacher responds, "Ah, enlightenment comes from good judgment." The student ponders for a moment and then asks, "Where does good judgment come from?" To which the teacher responds, "Experience." The student then asks the teacher, "Well—where does experience come from?" To which his wise teacher responds, "Bad judgment."

Like I said, no one is born wise. Wisdom is earned through having the courage to attempt things—and then learn from your mistakes. All "spiritual"-type teachers have come to teach to the world what they themselves need to learn. And I'm no exception.

My father said it best: "Success is what happens to you when and if you survive all your mistakes." As you will see in the coming chapters, I have made plenty of mistakes—several of which could have been lethal.

But here I am. I somehow survived. Now I'm sharing the experiences of my bad judgment with you, with the inten-tion to make your path to wisdom shorter and hopefully less painful than mine has been.

I've experienced so much self-inflicted pain in my life—a lot of it in my late teens and early to midtwenties—that I've set about making the rest of my life an attempt to lessen the pain of others and share the wisdom that I have learned.

In many ways, it was the pain of my bad judgment that led me to create *The Daily Love*. And my goal is to help my read-ers so much that one day, *The Daily Love* will itself become obsolete. The day the world no longer needs sites like *The Daily Love* will be a great day. It will mean we have embodied our essential spiritual wisdom so much that we take it as self-evident.

I often get asked, "How did you do it? How did you create something so incredible?" I could go on and on about the latest Internet marketing tools I use, social media strategies I've discovered, books I've read, or my Love of Jesus and His teachings. (I'll get to that last one later on, don't worry.) But I truly believe the foundation—why I was able to create something like *The Daily Love*, why I was able to overcome my addiction to drugs, why I've been able to clear all the seemingly insane hurdles that came and still come my way—is that I had solid parents.

my mom is one amazing woman

Throughout this book I will write about the many incredible teachers I have encountered. But the greatest teachers I have ever had are my parents.

I ultimately credit the Divine for all success, miracles, synchronicities, and happiness in my life. But my parents are the physical representation of that Divine Grace. They gave me the tools I needed to make it through the challenges of the world.

In their own unique way, each of my parents embodies key traits that I needed to make it in this lifetime.

My father and I both agree that my mother is one of the most dedicated, strong, resilient, passionate, incredible women we know. At the age of 14, she had an accident so severe she was lucky to have survived. She grew up on the East Coast and was an avid equestrian. She jumped horses competitively and was actually quite good at it. One fateful day, however, her horse reared up and threw her off. She landed on her back, square on a rock. Though she didn't know it then, that moment would define the rest of her life.

Mom didn't think anything of her injury for over a decade. But at the age of 28, the effects of the accident became clear. She was in pain so severe that something had to be done about it. She went to the doctor and they told her that by 40 she would be in a wheelchair. They said she would be in "level ten" pain for the rest of her life, and that she would certainly not have kids.

My mother has defied the odds her whole life, and she didn't take the doctors' prognosis at face value. Instead, she went on to have many operations on her back, including one where she died on the operating table and came back.

I am personally VERY grateful that she didn't give up, because if Mom had believed what the doctors told her, I would not be here today. So thank you, Mom, for following your intuition!

One of the core messages my mother always taught me was the idea that *your prognosis doesn't have be your diagnosis*. That is to say, the outcome of your life doesn't have to be what the experts tell you it's going to be. She also always said that her healing is 80 percent her responsibility and 20 percent the responsibility of the doctors.

I have watched her defy the medical odds for 32 years. The doctors she does work with have no idea how she's been able to do it, because her story has not turned out the way they thought it would.

Mom has had a steady yoga practice for many years, something we believe has played a massive part in her continued health. She is still not in a wheelchair. She did have kids—obviously. And she works toward lessening her pain every single day.

The year 2013 was a turning point in my mother's life. In June she gave up her position as editor at *The Daily Love* (a position she held since its beginning) to focus on her own healing. Around the same time I had invited her and my father to Los Angeles to spend some time with my girlfriend Jenna and me. I was always uncertain about whether Mom would be healthy enough to travel; her IBS often kept her from being able to. As the date approached, it became obvious that she couldn't make it. A few months later she couldn't make it to our Maui "Enter the Heart" retreat. And then a month after that she couldn't make it to an event I was doing in Kansas City for the "Enter the Heart" tour (only 20 miles from where she lived). I sat down with my mom, my dad, Jenna, and my dear friend Tommy Rosen and we decided it was time for my mom to go to rehab to get off the pain medication that she had been on for three decades. I wasn't sure if it was going to work. But after 45 days at the Betty Ford Center for pain management, my mother emerged a brand-new woman—both pain-free and smoke-free (she had also been a longtime smoker). I've never known my mother to be pain-free, and I never thought it would be possible in this lifetime. But, as of the writing of this book, my mother has been almost 80 days sober, and pain-free for about 40 days in a row. We spent Thanksgiving together with my parents and Jenna's parents and are already planning trips to Maui and Bali and all over the U.S.

I believe that kids pay far more attention to what their parents *do* than what their parents *say*. My mother never takes no for an answer. She is always trying to find a way. She never lets what other people think define what is possible for her. She doesn't just talk about things; she walks her talk. My mother's courage to go to rehab and her miracle story inspire me beyond words.

From her I've also learned that I can overcome any obstacle that might be put in my way through the power of my mind. All my life, Mom would reiterate that I could do anything I set my mind to. She said this so many times that she hypnotized me into actually believing it. It is this core belief that has carried me throughout my entire life. I literally believe there is nothing I can't do; that if I set my mind to something, I *can* figure it out.

What my mother *didn't* tell me was that sometimes it would be hard as hell. That sometimes you have to have many failures before success comes. But she prepared me to have an open and confident mind, without which I wouldn't have been able to overcome the challenges that came my way as I ventured out into the world.

what i learned from my dad

My father has also been an incredible source of inspiration, as well as a grounding force in my life. Dad served as a medic in the Vietnam War. While he lost many great friends in battle, he also served our country well and saved many people's lives. There are generations of families that owe their very existence to his efforts.

My father is one of the most curious people I know. He Loves life. In fact he is so fascinated by life that he decided to study it, literally—he has a Ph.D. in biology. (My mother is also a biologist—they are both *super* smart.) From an early age, he would teach me all kinds of fascinating things about the world and the way it works.

Since both of my parents are scientists, I was brought up with the scientific method as a cornerstone: Ask a question, do research, construct a hypothesis, test your hypothesis, analyze your data, and communicate the results. Then, do it all over again.

I've always seen life as an experiment. In my twenties I came by a quote from Ralph Waldo Emerson that resonated deeply with my upbringing and is now a guiding value in my life: "All life is an experiment. The more experiments you make the better."

Because the scientific process has been core to my thinking, I have always considered myself a "healthy, open-minded skeptic." This has been especially true (and beneficial) as I've made my way through the personal-growth world. There are so many claims about "what's possible," coming from all different healing modalities. Rather than taking the claims at face value, I am always testing these modalities to see if they work.

My parents raised me to have an open mind, but to test things. Most importantly, I learned to test my hypotheses and never accept claims on blind faith. Testing has been in my DNA since I was born. I've tested all kinds of different things, from drugs to spiritual teachers, diets to 12-step programs, and even possible love partners.

In fact, I see my whole world now as one giant test. I'm testing which ideas and healing modalities work best and which can be thrown away. I'm open to trying things at least once—and then having my own experience and making up my own mind.

What's so cool is that my parents actually respected me enough to *let* me make up my own mind. They never wanted me to conform to their views or what they thought I should be doing. They always gave me room to have my own experiences and respected me for the decisions I made.

I've had to carve out my own path in life. Many of the paths I found myself on ended up with other people telling me how to think. That's never worked for me. I'm basically unemployable; it's so hard for me to submit to authority. The good news is that, having been raised to be a healthy skeptic, I have understanding and compassion for those who are skeptical about *me*.

I believe that anyone who is a teacher of personal-growth material should be tested. As with any product, the "consumer" should be skeptical of teachers until they are proven trustworthy. This is a healthy and important part of the path.

My father taught me to kick the tires before you try anything new, but to be open to new ideas and beliefs. He taught me the core tenet of self-reliance, which is "Don't believe anything just because someone else said it; try it out for yourself." What I learned about being a healthy, open-minded skeptic as a child has guided my every step as I've gotten older.

Yoda and the Vulcans

One of the most formative experiences I had growing up was being introduced to both *Star Wars* and *Star Trek*. My parents are total geeks and are really into sci-fi. As a result I, too, became a geek—and never looked back. You could say that I am a child of the Force *and* Starfleet. Usually a person loves *Trek* more than *Wars* or *Wars* more than *Trek*—but I love them both so much, I can't imagine choosing.

I must have watched the original *Star Wars* movies over a hundred times. Even though it was science fiction, I was always fascinated with the concept of the Force. Whenever Yoda would talk of it—especially in *The Empire Strikes Back*, which I'll discuss in a later chapter—I felt the deep resonance of truth. I would dream of being Luke Skywalker and being able to "use" the Force for good.

I also grew up on *Star Trek: The Next Generation*. Captain Picard, Riker, Data, Troi, Worf, Geordi, Dr. Crusher, Guinan, and Wesley were my extended family. I was captivated by the idea of being able to travel the galaxy in a supercool ship with a group of people that all had each other's backs.

What I loved about *TNG* was that the episodes were about how to resolve conflict *without violence*. I was inspired by Gene Roddenberry's vision for the future: a time when we as human beings would see our oneness, instead of our differences—where we would know that each living being has intrinsic value.

One of my all-time favorite *Star Trek* moments was in the movie *First Contact*. It tells a story about an alien race called the Borg, and how they plot to take over the human race.

The Borg decide to travel back in time to when humans had first made contact with an alien race called the Vulcans. The Borg want to stop this "first contact" from happening, so they can use their advanced technology to conquer the human race and "assimilate" us.

Picard and crew follow the Borg back in time and have an epic battle with this fierce enemy. But the battle is not what's interesting to me. What's interesting is what happens when the good guys win.

The Borg were trying to stop the first manned spaceflight at warp speed, or the speed of light. They were unsuccessful, and as a result, a Vulcan ship that was flying through our solar system picked up the warp signature and decided to visit Earth.

Their arrival ushered in a whole new era of world peace, because human beings realized that we were not alone in the galaxy. This was a big deal, because the Vulcans arrived just after a third world war, when the planet was in ruin and humanity had no hope.

The first time I saw the Vulcans arrive on planet Earth and meet with human beings, I literally started to cry. It was as if some deep part of me really, really wanted this to happen.

I've always stared at the stars and wondered what's up there. I've always had a deep feeling that there is no way that we could be the only life in this big, vast Uni-verse. And I've also always felt a subtle yet deep pain for all the suffering on our planet. It seems so needless, this "us" versus "them" con-sciousness that we have. For all of our advanced technology, we are still a world of battling nations, tribal domination, and addiction—to power, money, oil, and many other things.

While growing up—and even now—the possibility that all the pain and suffering could come to an end truly moved me. I sometimes still get sad that I don't live in the Starfleet world. It seems like such a better place.

One of my driving desires is to have a deep sense of belonging. The first time I ever truly felt the feeling of belong-ing was because of *Star Trek*. The camaraderie of *Star Trek* still warms my heart to this day. In *Star Trek: The Next Gen-eration*, it felt like the crew was a family. They respected each other. They worked through problems together, and Captain Picard would always try to find a diplomatic rather than a military solution. I love to feel like I belong and to inspire others to feel like they belong as well. This is how we run the business of *The Daily Love* and also how we work with cli-ents. Belonging is the thread that informs our every move.

Later in life, I would use *The Empire Strikes Back* to find myself again. I'll tell you the full story in Chapter 5, but suf-fice to say at the time I had lost sight of what was important to me. I was deep in the grip of the entertainment industry in Los Angeles. It was while watching *Empire* for maybe the hundredth time, there in my apartment in LA, when I realized I was living in constant fear. Luke's journey into his own fear in *Empire* reminded me that hidden within all our fears is not some foreign, scary, far-off devil—but our truest self. When we face our fears, we are facing ourselves. There is no other "enemy"; all the fear we see in the world is an outward projection of the fear we have within us. Seeing the portrayal of such a profound truth at that time in my life was a big hint from the Uni-verse. It was as if the Uni-verse was saying, "Your fears, you must face them. Run no longer."

From that moment forward, things changed.

As I think about it now, the morals of *Star Trek* and *Star Wars* are a core part of my belief system. I fully believe in a sense of a global family and knowing there is a larger "Force" or "Divine" presence that connects and unites us all.

I know it seems strange to get one's morals from science fiction, but how many times has the science fiction of the past become today's reality?

the birth of a recovering Christian

Another thing my father gave me was a sense of faith in something larger than myself. He would take me to church every Sunday, where I learned about Christianity and the teachings of Jesus.

Every Sunday the pastor would talk about Love. Even then it seemed so obvious that core values like Love were true; it was amazing to me that we needed to talk about them. It's almost like having a sermon on the sun—talking about the sun as if we didn't see it right over our heads. I've since come to realize that many spiritual truths are not as self-evident to other people. As I've gotten older, I've begun to understand why. The farther we get from childhood, the more we seem to forget what we were born knowing—that Love is all there is and we are all connected to our Divine source.

That doesn't mean I always agreed with what the Church had to say. While I was brought up in the Church, I was also brought up with scientific parents who believed in evolution—which the Church did not. To me, the idea of evolution was normal and natural. It made sense that life evolves over time, getting better and better. That is the nature of life: to express itself and then improve upon its expression based on the results. In many ways, evolution is life—or the Uni-verse—using the scientific method. It has always seemed natural and intuitive to me.

That is, until I turned 13, when my church life and my school life collided. I had been born in Lawrence, Kansas, but we moved to Canada when I was 2. I lived there until I was about 10 years old and then we moved back to Lawrence. It was a hard time for me, integrating into the new school system. My parents were concerned about putting me into public school because of the gang problems at the time, and I moved schools several times trying to find the right fit.

I ended up going to a school in Topeka for a year, but I wanted a school that was closer to home and, more importantly, one that would allow me to play my favorite childhood sport—baseball. I was an avid baseball player and it meant everything for me to play in Little League. Douglas County Christian School was nearby, and in the district of the baseball league I wanted to play in, so I decided to go to DCCS. Plus, I thought it would be great to go to school with loving and faith-based people.

Unfortunately, what happened next would turn me away from my Christian faith for almost two decades.

One day I was in science class and we started learning about how the world was created. I was stunned to discover that my teacher, Mrs. Henry, was teaching not from a science book, but from the *Bible*. That day we learned the creation story in Genesis—you know, "In the beginning there was the Word, and the Word was with God . . ."

She went through what happened on the first day, the second day, and so on.

And when she was done she said, "And that is how God created the world."

She said it as a *fact*. It was so strange to me! I kept waiting for her to talk about evolution, to bring up how the world has been evolving for millions, if not *billions* of years.

So I raised my hand and asked her about evolution. She flat-out denied evolution existed. She said again that the world was created as God said it was—in the Bible.

It made no sense to my young scientific mind. I thought about it some more, and then raised my hand again. Because clearly—from my perspective—Mrs. Henry had her facts wrong.

"Mrs. Henry," I asked. "How old is this book?"

"About two thousand years old," she said.

"Right," I said. "And two thousand years ago, we didn't know what lightning was. We didn't understand gravity. We didn't understand much about life at all. We certainly didn't have science the way that we do today. Don't you think it's possible that the creation story in the Bible is a fable, told from very simple people to other very simple people, about how the world came into being? That perhaps it's a metaphor for evolution? Couldn't they be the same thing?"

Suffice to say that Mrs. Henry was stunned. My classmates were stunned. Mrs. Henry got so upset that she actually began to cry. I was so confused! I thought that I had brought up a very valid point. Instead of being rewarded for devising a theory that allowed for the coexistence of both creationism *and* evolution, I was ridiculed and sent to the principal's office!

What was worse was that the entire student body started making fun of me. They called me "monkey boy" from that day forward.

I was shocked. I thought that "Christians" were supposed to be kind, loving people who turned the other cheek. Yet I had never felt so judged or unloved in my entire life. I was done with God. I was done with Jesus. I was done with religion. If this is what Christianity meant, I didn't want any part of it.

It wasn't until almost two decades later that I realized there is a major difference between the Love of the Divine and the human beings who supposedly "represent" that Love. But at the age of 13 I got lost in the messenger—and missed the message of Christianity because of it.

journey to the dark side

That day began a long-term existential crisis in my life. I was so let down and so hurt (I didn't even know just *how* hurt at the time) that I turned away from all things "spiritual," "religious," or mystical for over a decade.

At the time, I didn't understand how massive the impact would be. Knowing what I know now—that all addictions come from a disconnection from Source, well-being, and our core Truth—I see that Mrs. Henry's class was the moment my life was set on the path of addiction.

From this moment forward, I went looking for "God" in all the wrong places.

I had no interest in going to church anymore and I started to sink myself into baseball, computer games, and a role-playing card game called Magic: The Gathering.

I dove heavily into metal music—my favorite bands growing up were Korn, Limp Bizkit, Slipknot, Sevendust, and Staind. But my all-time favorite to this day is Tool. Tool's sense of dark, melodic, and spiritual lyrics was how I found God in the days when I hated the version of God I had grown up with.

Even as I went through this stage of listening to music that—I can see now—was filled with anger, hate, and negative energy, my parents still supported me.

No matter what I was going through, or the music I was listening to, I was always Loved. I was Loved when I would blast (and I mean *blast*) Limp Bizkit all through the house. My parents would just ask me to turn it down, and I would.

They always honored my process and choices.

As destiny would have it, my good friend Tim became friends with the Limp Bizkit guys around 1997, right before they started getting huge. They had stopped in Lawrence on the Warped Tour. Tim sold comic books and vintage toys, and had a booth at the Warped Tour. Limp Bizkit's lead singer, Fred, loved toys and stopped by Tim's booth, and a friendship was born. We started going to all their concerts around the country.

So here I am, a high school kid in Kansas, and I'm traveling around the country on weekends to see Limp Bizkit play in Dallas, Chicago, LA, and NYC. It was like I was living some nu-metal version of *Almost Famous*. Kids at school would ask me what I did over the weekend, but when I told them I was hanging out on tour with LB, they didn't believe me. So I kept my travels to myself.

We got to go backstage at the shows and we always came bearing gifts, like limited edition toys. LB's first album was called *Three Dollar Bill, Y'all*, and we made limited edition three-dollar bills with Limp Bizkit logos on it for the band. This was an early lesson for me: when you add value to other people's lives, cool things happen.

One night that stands out: Tim and I were at Limp Bizkit's sold-out concert at the Bronco Bowl in Dallas right when their single "Nookie" was number one around the world. Staind and Kid Rock were opening. Afterward, Tim and I joined the band on the bus, where everyone was celebrating the number-one record—they'd even beat out the massively popular Backstreet Boys. There I was, a 17-year-old from Kansas partying with my favorite band the week their record went to number one! It was a dream come true. And it also showed me what was possible, which wouldn't have happened if my parents hadn't given me the freedom to explore.

That night, I met a man who was introduced to me as the band's manager. I got to know him and asked if he was looking for interns. "Always," he said. So I told him I was moving to LA soon and would work for him for free. (By the way, I had *no* plans to move—I just made it up on the spot.) He gave me his card and then he left.

I didn't realize until much later how that single moment of opportunity would change my life. It would be the beginning of a time that would show me the great and amazing possibilities of life—as well as the dark depths of addiction.

Both would be great teachers for me, even though the darkness would almost kill me.

But what I see looking back is that it all was made possible by my parents. I really cannot begin to express my gratitude to them for allowing me to choose what kind of life I wanted to live. Now that I know the kind of negative effects parents can have on their children, I see how lucky I was to get my mom and dad. I feel totally blessed.

They tried for a long time to give me a fairy-tale childhood. And while I was raised with great innocence that remains with me today, perhaps I would have benefited from a little more reality, too. As it was, over the next few years I got the education in pain my parents had sheltered me from—and then some.

As I got into my addictions—and as I got seduced by money, power, and fame—I would lose myself for a time. Upon reflection, it reminds me of the movie *Labyrinth*. The character Sarah is on her way to the Goblin City, when she's betrayed by her friend Hoggle—he gives her poisonous fruit and she falls asleep.

In this sleep, it seems like life is wonderful. She is in a fancy ballroom that would satisfy any young girl's wildest dreams. But in this illusion, Sarah forgets who she is.

My journey into Hollywood would put me to sleep for some time. I would lose myself. I would give away my power. I would go to some of the darkest places that a human being can go.

But I would emerge wiser for it.

I, like Luke Skywalker, had to go into the darkness to face myself. That is where my journey was taking me—far beyond any place I felt comfortable, into the depths of what I feared most.

I would come to find a Joseph Campbell quote much later in life that put it all into perspective: "The very cave you are afraid to enter turns out to be the source of what you are looking for."

Darkness was coming, but I didn't know it. Yet as I said good-bye to my amazing parents and headed off to LA, I was excited to welcome whatever adventures were coming next.

— chapter 3 —

ADVENTURES IN HOLLYWOODLAND

"But I don't want to go among mad people," Alice remarked. "Oh, you can't help that," said the Cat: "we're all mad here. I'm mad. You're mad." "How do you know I'm mad?" said Alice. "You must be," said the Cat, "or you wouldn't have come here."

—LEWIS CARROLL,
ALICE IN WONDERLAND

It takes a certain type of person to leave the confines of their comfortable life and venture out into the unknown. It's not an easy thing to do. It takes courage and determination, because there are bound to be a lot of setbacks along the way. In fact, journeying into the deep unknown is one of the hardest things we can ever choose to do.

I didn't realize this when I set my sights on leaving Kansas and moving to Hollywood.

At the time all I knew was what my mother had always told me: "You can do anything you put your mind to." Which is some of the best advice I ever got, because if I didn't actually believe I could do whatever I wanted, I don't think I would have been naïve enough—or perhaps crazy enough—to actually move to Hollywood. It would have been so easy to stay at home and take the path that was laid out before me: college, job, family. And if I had done that, you probably wouldn't be reading my book right now.

Lucky for me, deep down I knew I wasn't going to be happy taking the traditional route. It seemed too predictable. So moving to LA didn't require a second thought for me. It was the only option. Tim and I had traveled to LA when I was 16, and there I got my first tattoo and smoked pot for the second time ever. On that trip I saw Danny Glover at a hotel, and that was all it took. I wanted to be in the land of celebrity. I wanted to make my mark. I wanted to live where there was the best weather and the most beautiful women in the world. I wanted to be at the top of a town the whole world was watching.

Things didn't go according to plan, though. My *plan* was to come to LA as a freshman in college. I was going to attend the University of Southern California in their Music Industry program. I was going to become a child prodigy of the music biz, managing all my favorite bands and getting a front-row seat at every concert I ever wanted to go to, not to mention the Grammys and the MTV Video Music Awards. I had no intention of actually *finishing* college, mind you—USC would just be my ticket to LA, the way to get my parents' blessing. I knew that once I got to town, everything would change. I didn't know how it would change or what it would change into, but I knew that it would change. I felt I had a destiny in Los Angeles. I yearned to be included in something really important, and Hollywood felt like just the place.

But it didn't turn out that way, because I got rejected from USC. And I went to the University of Kansas instead.

It was a setback, but it didn't kill my dream. I just had to try again. Unfortunately, I couldn't reapply for a whole year. That was a painful year, because I knew I didn't belong at KU. All I could think about was getting into USC. I doubled my efforts and applied again for my sophomore year.

The day I got the acceptance letter from USC was one of the most exciting days of my life. I knew from that moment forward life would never be the same again. It was one of the first times I can remember the Uni-verse really saying YES to my dreams.

So there I was. I had my ticket to LA, entry to USC, and one—just one—very important contact in the music business: Paul.

Paul was the music manager I'd met on the Limp Bizkit tour bus years before. From the moment I met him I'd set my sights on working for him—and climbing the Hollywood music business ladder from there. As destiny would have it, I ran into Paul at the Roxy on the Sunset Strip a month after moving to LA in the summer of 2001. I don't think it would have happened this way had I moved a year earlier. Looking back at this moment it seemed like total Divine guidance—a "Godshot," as I like to say.

When I saw Paul across the room at the Roxy I knew this was my chance. But I was so nervous that I first bribed the bartender to give me a shot of Jägermeister (I was 19). With that, I muscled up the courage to go and talk to Paul.

To my surprise, he remembered me—and he remembered where we met. It was awesome. I told him I was ready to be his intern, to work for free, and to kick some ass. The timing was perfect: it was a Saturday in August, and his summer intern had just left to go back to NYC the day before. I started on Monday.

Total Godshot. Total Divine synchronicity. Right?

For the second time that year, I felt like the Uni-verse was giving me a big YES on what I wanted to do with my life. I'd had two back-to-back confirmations that things were going according to plan. I couldn't believe it. For years I had dreamed of coming to LA and playing with the big shots. And here I was, about to start my journey with the very "big shot" who happened to manage one of my favorite bands.

Could this really be possible?

YES. Life was showing me—it *is* possible for dreams to come true.

I was talking it over with a friend later in the week, and he said it was just like Woody Allen said: "Showing up is 80 percent of life." I hadn't heard that quote before but I've never forgotten it. Because the magic I was experiencing really was from just that—showing up. I decided that, from that moment forward, I would start really showing up for life. Because if *this* had just happened, what else was possible?

no is not an option

I once heard Marianne Williamson say that you can learn through pain, or you can learn through joy. As it turns out, painful lessons sometimes look like getting exactly what you want.

Things were happening for me. I hadn't just ended up in some ragtag management shop—I had landed at the number one name in music management in Hollywood. I was so green I had no idea just how prestigious the company was until I was already firmly entrenched there.

Paul, someone whom I love dearly to this day, became my first mentor in the business. But he also became a major figure on my spiritual journey. He'd never taken an Abraham-Hicks workshop, but this man was a true master; if you could think it, Paul could manifest it. Under his tutelage, I learned how to make almost anything happen, almost anywhere in the world.

I was amazed at what Paul could do. He was working not just with Limp Bizkit but about four or five other major bands. The man would orchestrate worldwide tours, while making multimillion-dollar records, while helping his friends get through rehab, while being in a relationship, while maintaining a healthy social life.

The amount to which Paul was living life inspired me. I can remember sitting in his office as an intern, staring in bewilderment (and somewhat awkwardly) as he would take phone call after phone call, all day long. He was the supreme organizer of many people's lives. He was the best music manager I've ever seen. If his clients wanted it done, it didn't matter how big or small, Paul was there to do it.

I was so inspired by the power that Paul wielded that I wanted to soak it up. At the office I was the first one in and the last one out every day. I did everything I was asked to do without hesitation. I found out that in Hollywood having good Midwestern ethics—like saying you are going to do something and then doing it—goes really far. Woody Allen was right; I just kept showing up and things kept happening.

I loved the power I had, interning at such an influential company. There wasn't a desire a client had that we wouldn't make come true. Concerts, spontaneous flights, food from a restaurant in New York delivered to an artist's doorstep in LA. It didn't matter what it was, we could manifest it. We could coordinate a worldwide tour or negotiate a massive contract in a week or less. "No" was not in our vocabulary. Paul drilled into my head to never accept no for an answer. That no matter how much resistance I got from the world, it was my job to get the job done.

One of Paul's core mantras was "Never give work back to your boss." This taught me to be on my game and to think for myself. I would listen to Paul on the phone, watch how he worked, see how he made things happen—and then do it like he did. Later I learned from Tony Robbins that this is called "modeling," but at that point I called it "I want to be just like Paul."

Coming from Kansas, and having had very little power most of my life, I started to crave more of it. The people who worked at our company were respected by everyone in the industry. They were talking with all the top radio and press people, creating sold-out concerts all over the world. Just being around them I started to believe that I was invincible— that I could do whatever I wanted. I started to think I was better than everyone else.

I also started to judge my former life. I started seeing my former self as a loser, and I thought the people from my hometown were losers, too. In my eyes, everyone had low standards compared to the level of excellence I saw in Hollywood. On any given day, greed, power, and the desire to be well-known all over the world coursed through my body. I decided that if I had to sell my soul to be powerful in Hollywood, I would do it. Looking back, I can see I would have thrown my own mother under a bus if it meant gaining more power and influence.

And then there were the drugs. In the world of Hollywood, glitz, glam, and drugs go hand in hand. Very quickly I started living my own *E! True Hollywood Story*. In order to keep up with the hours and fit into the fast Hollywood lifestyle, I developed a heavy cocaine habit. I had only touched drugs a few times in high school, but here I was justifying my behavior because it fit in with the scene all around me. I began to wake up and do cocaine, simultaneously taking Xanax throughout the day to calm my stress. Then I would ramp up the cocaine at night so I had enough energy to go out. Night after night, almost seven days a week, I would fall asleep—thanks to even more Xanax—as the sun was rising. At my lowest I needed to set five different alarms in order to wake up and slept just a couple of hours a night.

I was going to the right parties and working at the right company—so of course I needed the right car. At the time I was driving an old 3 Series BMW I'd found back in Lawrence. It was old and I got it dirt cheap, but it was a BMW—*the* car to drive in LA. One day as I was driving to work I rolled my driver's-side window down and it got stuck. When I couldn't roll it back up, I got impatient. But instead of fixing it, I called the BMW dealership, had them pick up my old BMW as a trade-in, leased a brand-new BMW, and had it delivered to the office that same day. It made more sense to my cocaine-brain to do this than to just get the car window fixed.

The new BMW ended up being a big mistake. I got stuck with a $500-a-month lease that I soon could not afford. I was about to become the guy in LA with the nice car but not much else—though I didn't know it then. At that point all that mattered was that I had the right ride to go with the right parties, the right job, and the right drugs. I was on the rise in the industry, I told myself. I needed to stay up until 2 or 3 A.M. so I could make calls to the U.K.! If that meant I had to sniff some lines in the morning along with my coffee, then so be it. It got so bad that I started crushing Adderall and mixing it with the coke, and that was my wake-up drug of choice.

But the fast life was catching up with me. I started needing drugs at the office just to stay awake and focused. The thing about cocaine is that it wears on your nose. I started having daily nosebleeds from the cocaine, so I had to swab my nose with vitamin E every night. I started taking Pedialyte (which hydrates the system) to counteract my incessant drinking, and downed Advil to stay ahead of the inevitable hangover each morning. I was going downhill—and fast.

how to blow your dream job in less than a month

Somehow I made it through for about two years, abusing my body all the while. I was still at USC but all my attention was on my internship. Then the Uni-verse upped the ante in the form of an opening for my dream job: senior vice president of A&R (the talent scout division that is responsible for finding and discovering new artists and repertoire) for Limp Bizkit's lead singer, Fred Durst, at his record label, Flawless, an imprint of Geffen Records. Even though I knew I couldn't do the job and go to school at the same time, I applied. I had worked so hard for one of the bands Paul managed on the Flawless label that they suggested me for the job. Lo and behold, I got it.

There I was, at the tender age of 21, in a position guys twice my age would have killed for. I was thrilled. The night before I started, I was hanging out at Fred's house and he said, "Mastin, the only way you can mess up this job is if you take too many drugs." Could he see I was headed for trouble? Was he psychic? Or was he just messing with my head? I wasn't sure, and suffice to say I didn't listen.

In a matter of a few weeks I had dropped out of USC, signed a six-month lease on an apartment next door to the Geffen offices in Santa Monica . . . and gotten fired.

Yes, you heard that right.

There were a few reasons I got fired. I was doing all the wrong things. First and foremost I was doing drugs in the office all day long. (As far as I know they never found out about that—sorry, Fred.) The massive amount of drugs I was taking clearly affected my judgment and ability to be a part of the team. I wasn't good at understanding the different politics of being at a label versus being at a management company, so I stepped on a lot of toes. I didn't play well with the guys upstairs, caused a fuss I can't tell you about because I signed a non-disclosure agreement about it, and got the boot.

Now here I was, freshly 22, strung out on drugs, and fired from my dream job. I felt like Hollywood had chewed me up and spit me out. It was as if all I had dreamed about and worked toward was over.

For a couple of weeks after I got fired, I stayed in my apartment and did what I did best: drank and did drugs. I shut everyone out, and was drowning in my own shame for having failed. I felt like I'd let myself and my parents down. I now believe a small sliver of my consciousness, one that dwelt deep down inside of me, knew that my challenging circumstances were for the best. I think I knew that everything would be okay eventually, but in the moment I was heavily depressed, deeply sad, and even contemplating suicide. At some point I realized I had also let God down, even though my idea of Him was foggy and unformed.

And yet even during this dark, terrible period of my life, Grace still visited me. The first defining moment occurred at about 3:30 A.M. on a Sunday morning. I was in the San Fernando Valley, driving back to Santa Monica from my girlfriend's house in Sherman Oaks. There were almost no other cars on the road, but when I pulled out onto the street, I somehow managed to cut someone off.

Someone driving a POLICE CAR.

Thankfully I had not been drinking that night. (I was stupid, but not stupid enough to drink and drive.) That said, I did have a stash of cocaine under my seat. When the cops pulled me over, I offered to take a Breathalyzer test but they didn't take me up on it. I apologized and explained to them I was tired and was heading home, and they let me off the hook. My heart was beating very hard. If I had gotten caught with that cocaine in the car, it would have meant jail time. Worse yet (for me), total industry humiliation.

As I headed for home, I suddenly felt a presence in the car with me. It was one of the first instances I remember *feeling* my intuition. There were no bright lights, and there was no visual, just a deep knowing that this was a warning and next time I wouldn't be so lucky. For the first time, I realized I had to get sober. I knew I was meant for more than the fear- and pain-filled existence I was leading. I wanted to quit drugs, but I kept putting it off "until tomorrow." I knew that my next brush with danger would not be as Grace-filled as this one had been.

And yet, in typical addict style, I kept on using. As the reality of my job loss sank in—and as my relationship started to crumble and my entire life started to come down around me—I isolated myself and dove deeper into the drugs and drinking. I didn't know what was happening to me; I just felt like life was against me. I started having heart palpitations on top of everything else. I could actually feel my heart skipping beats when my second defining moment occurred.

It was a few weeks after I had cut off the police car. I had been doing cocaine all night, not to mention drinking a full bottle of red wine and taking Viagra. (Someone had told me it would make me feel high.) I remember my heart was racing and my face turned red. I was cutting up another line of coke when I suddenly felt the same presence I'd felt in the car that night in Sherman Oaks.

If you do that line you're cutting up right now, a voice told me, *you'll die.*

I wish I could say that was enough to stop me, but the truth was that my arrogant addict voice drowned out the voice of that presence. I kept on cutting the line. I believed I was invincible, but as I bent down to sniff it, I found I couldn't do it. It felt as if another being had taken over my body. No matter how much I wanted that line, I couldn't do it. It felt like my conscious mind was not in control anymore. Was it cocaine psychosis? Maybe. I like to think it was the presence of God's Grace.

Whatever it was, this energy directed me to get up and throw out the coke and all the other drugs in my house, which I did. As I flushed it all down the toilet, part of me couldn't believe what I was doing. But a wiser part of me knew a Holy presence was preventing me from doing any further damage to myself. This was very strange because I'm not a "woo-woo" kind of guy. I was raised by scientists, after all. But I'm telling you exactly what happened.

Years later, when I reflected on that moment during a meditation, I saw an image of Christ entering my body, stopping me from taking what could have been a lethal action. I now believe that the Christ presence entered my body in that moment—a moment of pure Divine Grace that saved my life. Of course, there's no way to know whether I would have lived or died if I had done that line, but I can tell you this much: it did get my attention.

I did cocaine because, for a short time, it gave me a heightened sense of self-esteem and the ability to focus REALLY well. I was doing the best I could to increase my productivity and my sense of self. I didn't have better tools or resources at my disposal at the time.

Upon reflection of my own addictions, I've come to believe that the addict is someone who is looking for God in all the wrong places.

After I cleaned up, I started asking myself, "How can I feel good about myself—feel good in my body and learn to focus so I can get stuff done—*without* drugs?" My goal became to feel as good off the drugs as I'd felt on them. Tony Robbins (a mentor of mine who you will meet later in the book) says that the quality of our lives is based on the quality of the questions we ask. The above question is vitally important to me and the way I live, even to this day. I'm still seeking answers to it. But being able to ask it at all was a major step for me—one which soon led me to the teachings of an amazing woman named Caroline Myss, whom I'll tell you more about in the next chapter.

But my immediate takeaway from that period was that getting what you want can sometimes be a horrible stroke of luck. I had no idea what I was getting myself into when I came to Hollywood, and I wasn't prepared for what happened to me. I was just a kid looking to go on an adventure. What I ended up with was an almost lethal addiction. All I'd wanted was to be someone in the music business. While that came true for a brief moment, it was not worth the price of admission. Hollywood brought out the worst in me. The Grace of that experience is that I got to see some pretty amazing things before I lost access. I saw how bands launched multiplatinum records. I saw how movies were made and released. I saw how brands were created. I saw how the wizards pull all the strings. In therapy years later I would ask God, *Why did you show me the greatness of Hollywood and then take it all away?* I've had to live that question for many years, but I've come to believe that I was being prepared for who I was to become.

— chapter 4 —

TAKING MY
POWER BACK

*Managing the power of choice, with all its creative and
spiritual implications, is the essence of the human
experience. All spiritual teachings are directed toward
inspiring us to recognize that the power to make choices
is the dynamic that converts our spirits into matter, our
words into flesh. Choice is the process of creation itself.*

—CAROLINE MYSS,
ANATOMY OF THE SPIRIT

WHEN YOU ASK, THE UNI-VERSE RESPONDS—ESPECIALLY
when it's a deep ask from your heart. Once I asked to feel
as good off the drugs as I did on them, the strangest things
started happening to me—and not in the way I might have
expected.

After crashing and burning in the music business, I decided
to open up shop myself. I started my own music management
company, and it took off. Very quickly I was managing all
kinds of bands—a folk singer, a hard rock band, an alt band.

But even though I had some success, my energy and passion were gone. After a while it felt like I was beating a dead horse. I wasn't a manager because I loved what I was doing; I was a manager because I didn't know what else to do.

I've come to believe that the Divine speaks to you in languages that you can understand. While I wasn't going to church, wasn't surrounding myself with spiritual folks, and wasn't doing yoga, miracles still began happening in my life.

And, as usual, the miracles didn't look like miracles at first.

One day a client came to me and said I should manage his friend's band, Aeon Spoke. I wasn't interested in taking on any more clients, but when I heard the band's music and message, I found myself saying yes. I didn't know why, but I knew I had to do something with them. Aeon Spoke was an alternative rock band, yet they had a vibe that was almost sacred.

They proceeded to change my life. Not because they became a massive Grammy Award–winning client, but because they led me to my next Godshot.

Aeon Spoke had a song called "Emmanuel," which was being featured in the film *What the Bleep Do We Know!?*, about how spirituality and quantum physics go hand in hand. It paved the way for films like *The Secret*. I wasn't into spiritual films at all—at the time they seemed like a strange departure from my loves, *Star Wars* and *Star Trek*. But the movie was catching on, and the filmmakers were hosting *What the Bleep* screenings around LA. When the band was invited to perform at one of those screenings, I decided to go. It was weird—I didn't know why, but I felt like something was going to change for me forever because of that event.

I assumed I would meet my soul mate. (At the time I was constantly trying to find "The One.") That did not happen. But what *did* happen was incredible. I was introduced to the next important mentor in my life.

It was February 4th, 2005. The event was taking place at the Loews Santa Monica Beach, which is an upscale hotel. That helped me relax; it seemed too fancy a venue to host anything too "woo-woo."

Little did I know. When I got there it was all crystal balls, aura photographs, energy readings, tarot cards, and astrology charts—in other words, not my scene. At all. From the moment I walked in I decided there was no way that I was going to get anything from these "crazy" people. But as I was soon to discover, the Divine knows exactly how to talk to us.

There just happened to be a very cute girl working the "aura photography" booth.

I didn't know what an aura was, or how you could photograph it, but I knew I wanted to talk to *her*. I quickly decided she was the reason I had felt called to attend this strange gathering. So I went up and asked all about aura photography and what it was. I got my photo taken (still didn't understand what I was seeing) and then asked for her phone number.

Let's just say she didn't give me her number. But what she *did* give me would alter the course of my life forever: a CD set called *Energy Anatomy* by the spiritual teacher Caroline Myss.

I believe that when you are open to life and not attached to how your blessings show up, you are led to exactly what you need. Literally, you will encounter the exact CD set, book,

DVD, or USB drive that carries the message you most need to hear. The key is to not judge the source. Here I was, thinking I was going to meet my wife (or at least girlfriend) at this event. Instead I got a self-help CD. (Great. Thanks, God.)

On the surface, it looked like a loss. But I had actually gained an opportunity to go deeper.

my spiritual midwife

For those of you who have never encountered Caroline Myss's work, let me tell you two things. First, her last name is pronounced "mace," as in the self-defense spray. Second, her voice and tone match that pronunciation.

Her message, on the other hand, really worked for me. I'm not into the "woo," as I've said. You know what I'm talking about—angels, crystals, tarot, astrology, etc. I know I'm not going to be entirely popular for saying this, but I consider these modalities to be "spiritual entertainment"—screens we can project our spiritual hopes and dreams onto. Human beings have a thing called confirmation bias, where we tend to find what we go looking for. I've just encountered too many charlatans to take these modalities seriously. They may entertain us, but in the end they aren't grounded in anything tangible.

So I'm not big on spiritual entertainment. To me, it's no different than going to a movie. You may get a temporary emotional catharsis, but when you leave the movie what do you have? A bloated stomach and popcorn regret. Sure—you get to feel some feelings, but when you wake up the next day nothing has changed because you haven't taken any *action*. People think they know something because they understand a concept, but I believe you don't know something until you are doing it. It's great to be inspired, but it's all spiritual entertainment unless you *do* something with your new insights and inspirations.

Well, Caroline Myss is not the spiritual entertainment type. She means business. When I popped *Energy Anatomy* into my CD player, the first thing that struck me was her voice. Put nicely, it commands attention and respect. It was as if my mother had gone to nun school, left it to become a mystic, then joined the armed forces, and graduated as a drill sergeant. Caroline wanted me to wake up more than anything, and that meant I couldn't get away with any of the nonsense I had been taking part in (i.e., drugs, alcohol, and pretending like I didn't have an obligation to live my purpose). She had my number, and I was grateful. Below the tough-love façade I could feel a big heart wanting me—and all of humanity—to wake up to the beautiful power each of us has to make *choices*. You see, Caroline explains that choice is the fundamental way that we use our power. The way that we choose to live our lives determines so much. Everything you are thinking, wearing, doing, and believing is a reflection of a choice you've made either consciously or subconsciously. When we begin to analyze the choices in our lives and why we make them, we wake up to a larger understanding of ourselves and our priorities.

Caroline was my bridge—the exact voice I needed to re-enter the spiritual path I had abandoned after my experiences in Christian school. I had turned my head and my heart away from God for years, but Caroline brought me back by speaking a language I could understand.

She didn't lay down a lot of dogma; instead she put the responsibility back onto me. You see, so much of the religion I had grown up with was all about rules to please some sky god. Caroline got me to understand that there is no sky god and that only when I take responsibility for my life and my choices will I experience "Heaven on Earth." She wasn't telling me to trust the angels; she was making sure I knew how to make the best choices possible *myself*. Soon enough I discovered that I had been using my power in all the wrong ways.

Specifically, I had been giving it over to external sources— that's the nature of addiction. As Caroline says, "Addiction is the lack of a developed will. You've given your will over to an external source that has authority over your biology, your psychology." This was such a powerful concept for me; I had never thought about addiction that way.

I had relinquished my will—that is to say, my ability to choose. I'd given substances authority over me. I didn't like the idea that anything had authority over me, but I had to admit it was true. This is what they mean in the 12-Step tradition of Alcoholics Anonymous when they say that you are "powerless" over your addiction.

I dove deeper into Caroline's work to find out how to take my will back. I thought it would be an easy one-two punch; make a new choice and then all is well. This wasn't the case. I am still working on taking back my power to this day. In fact,

I've come to believe it's a daily spiritual practice. But there's no doubt I took massive leaps toward getting a handle on my will thanks to Caroline's work.

In *Energy Anatomy*, Caroline breaks down the energy centers of the body—called chakras—and explains each chakra's meaning or learning lesson. From her perspective, all life is a lesson about how to direct your will, and our chakras hold the map.

your tribe and your sexual energy: first and second chakras

As I dove deeper into Caroline's work, I began to understand my relationship to each of my seven chakras. I could see how I was holding myself back from living a fully expressed life (i.e., standing directly in my own way), and how I needed to change.

Energy Anatomy starts with our first chakra (what I like to call the "butt chakra"), which deals with our identification with "the tribe." In other words, how the energy is flowing through this chakra impacts whether and how your tribe has power over you.

Your tribe could be your friends, family, or business community—any group of people you associate with. By studying the concept of the first chakra, I learned that I had to step away from tribal "approval" and learn to do what *I* wanted to do, regardless of what others thought. I had been really good at this as a child, but as I matured (and got into the music business, aka the game of money, power, and fame) I lost my own compass.

I started to see how my deep need to "be someone" had brought me into the music business in the first place and ruled my behavior once I got there. Even after I had been ejected, I still wanted to prove "them" wrong. I had started my own management company to prove that I wasn't a mess-up. I had to face the hard truth that addiction, arrogance, and naïveté had caused me to fall from Grace and I was doing everything I could to stand up again. I wasn't willing to face the truth: that I had failed. I had messed up and I had egg on my face in the industry.

My dream of coming to Hollywood had turned into a nightmare, and I couldn't deal with that. Through Caroline's work I started to see that there was something else that I wanted to do. Though at the time I was unsure what that was, I knew it likely had nothing to do with the music business.

Unfortunately, I was so locked into the need for tribal approval that it felt impossible to quit. I didn't want to be perceived as a failure. I didn't want to admit that I was down and out. So I started to ask a new question: *What would I do if I didn't need the approval of the music business?*

The answer came, and I didn't like it. I had this overwhelming sense that *I was supposed to bring inspiration to the world.* I didn't have a vision, an angel didn't swoop down and tell me what I needed to do. It was just a deep knowing from within that the next phase of my evolution would include sharing with others what I had learned about personal growth. This knowing became louder and louder inside my head, until I couldn't ignore it anymore.

Nothing could have sounded sillier to me at the time. The last thing I wanted was to be some cheesy, snake oil salesman self-help guy with bad style, giving boring lectures while failing to practice what I was preaching.

I remember trying to barter with the Divine.

"I'll do anything *but* that," I would say in my prayers.

I wasn't ready to accept my calling, so I kept on with my pursuits in the music business. Things got better—and then they got worse. (More on that later.)

Luckily I was still listening to *Energy Anatomy*. Soon Caroline moved on to the second chakra. Your second chakra corresponds to your junk—your genitals. It represents sexual energy, creative energy, and money. (At its essence, money is a form of creative energy.) As I reviewed my life, I saw that I hadn't written or been creative since high school. I had spent most of my money on drugs and my other addictions—sugar, gambling, power, prestige, and many other dark choices. Like many young men in their twenties, I had a very hard time containing and focusing my sexual energy. In other words, when I looked over my life, I saw that the majority of my second-chakra energy was being wasted. I was using this life force in all the wrong ways: spending money I didn't have to impress others, filling my body with all kinds of substances that distracted me from feeling my feelings, chasing girls I had no place chasing, and putting all my creative energy into keeping up with the music business Joneses. Luckily, after I'd gotten fired, there was a long period where money seemed to run away from me. Looking back at my life, I believe that this was ultimate Grace. If I had had real money at that time I likely would have killed myself with drugs and alcohol. When I realized how I had been using my second-chakra energy, I saw that the decision to feel good *off* drugs had been a powerful reclamation of this part of my body.

I look at the death of Cory Monteith, the talented star of *Glee* who died of a drug overdose in 2013. He was born in May of 1982, just a couple months after me. His fate could have easily been mine; for a long time I was on the exact same path.

self-esteem, the heart, and willpower: the third, fourth, and fifth chakras

I thought the worst of the realizations was behind me, but soon I was moving up Caroline's chakra system to the third chakra, located at the solar plexus (aka your tummy). This energy center represents our self-esteem and self-love. Suddenly I was having painful insights of a whole different variety! The sad truth is that I've never really loved my body, and my self-esteem has been heavily impacted for most of my life by the fact that I've been overweight. Surprise, surprise, I carry my extra weight in my belly—the third chakra area.

At the time, the concept of self-love seemed so foreign to me that I thought it was actually selfish and narcissistic to love yourself. I spent all my time as a music manager loving other people and ignoring my own self-care. I was in codependent relationships with my clients and my love interests. Nowadays I wholeheartedly believe in self-love, while also recognizing that love is only complete once it's extended to others—but back then I didn't get it at all.

What Caroline taught me was that there is a difference between being selfish and being "self-ish." Selfishness is being just focused on you—totally narcissistic. Being *self-ish*, on the other hand, is being able to set good boundaries, focusing on your self-care and yet not making your life a selfish life. A self-ish person fills themselves up so they can serve others in greater and greater ways. It means being in your power— being fully yourself.

Caroline also taught me that there is no self-help without self-acceptance. At the time, I had none. I felt invisible, like I didn't matter. I also saw that there were so many different people's opinions that I valued over my own.

Just as outside substances had authority over me, the approval of others had authority over me as well: my ex-girl-friend, my ex-bosses Paul and Fred, my current clients, and that damned voice of self-hate within me. I was seeking approval everywhere but my own heart.

Whenever I wanted to try something new, all these voices would rise up in my head and try to tell me what I should or shouldn't do. *What would Paul think? What would Mom or Dad do in this same situation? What makes you think you deserve to succeed?*

On top of that, I was horrible at setting boundaries. I would give and give and give and give with no regard for my own needs. It had to do with the business I was in. In the music business—and entertainment in general—there is no such thing as a boundary. If you are an assistant, you are expected to be there for your boss. Always. It doesn't matter if it's the middle of the night, the wee hours of the morning, the weekend, or even Christmas. You are expected to be there, and be *fully* there, whenever your boss calls. Any sign of setting a boundary and you're "not a team player." This was mostly because our bosses had no boundaries with their clients, and they passed the work on to their employees.

As fun and flashy as the entertainment business can be—and for all the magical work that comes out of Hollywood—I do think the industry has a lot to learn about how to treat people. It's a dark business in a lot of ways, where approval addiction and codependency are rampant.

In order to fit in, I abandoned myself to earn the approval of those above me. I've since learned that you should never abandon yourself to please another. But that was a lesson I had to learn, and Caroline started the ball rolling for me.

I believe that Life, the Uni-verse, or the Divine *wants* us to be seen. So we will be seen, one way or another. Many times third-chakra issues stem from not speaking our truth because we want to be liked. We abandon ourselves in order to get approval. When this happens, our third chakra is affected. Our poor sense of self may manifest as poor digestion and/or over-eating, which is ironic, because our waistlines start to expand; although we're unwilling to "show ourselves" through speaking up and allowing our truth to be known, our bodies get bigger and bigger until we can't help but be seen.

Instead, we must ask ourselves, *Whose approval would I need in order to speak up?* and *What's the worst thing that would happen if I spoke my truth?* While many of us hide ourselves to avoid feeling abandoned, in truth all abandonment from others begins when we abandon ourselves.

Once we start to have a sense of self, the fourth chakra—also called the heart chakra—can begin to open. The fourth chakra is located in the center of your chest, just to the right of your physical heart. I've come to believe that the Heart is truly the wise center of the body; its wisdom is far superior to that of the mind's intellect. In fact, I believe that the Heart is the spark of the Divine within you. It's literally the location where God resides within you. In my one-on-one mentoring and in the seminars I offer all over the world, I practice something I call Kipp Heart Therapy. KHT is a practice of talking to your heart to find clarity, strength, and direction. (For more on KHT, visit DailyLove.com/KHT.)

When I first came across Caroline Myss's work, I didn't know a thing about the Heart. As a child of two scientists, I worshipped the mind. If you'll forgive another *Star Trek* reference, I was kind of like a Vulcan. I suppressed my emotions and had no understanding of Heart-based intuition.

Caroline says the truth of the fourth chakra is, "Love is Divine Power." What does this mean? It means your Soul and the whole Uni-verse stems from the energy of Love. We tend to forget this in a world drenched in fear and the resulting cortisol and adrenaline that leaves our body almost incapable of perceiving the subtler energy of Love. But Love is the communication vessel of the Divine. When we truly act on Love, when we embody Love and lead with it, the whole Uni-verse conspires to aid us in our work. It's virtually impossible to get there through the mind, but once we tap into our Heart we begin to feel our way. In fact, Joseph Campbell has said that the whole point of life and the Hero's Journey is for *"the Heart to usher the mind into the zone of revelation."*

Caroline teaches that we can use the Heart to help guide us through difficult circumstances of all varieties. For example, she teaches that we can pray for people who trigger us by saying: *"Let me learn more about how to love them today."*

She also taught me that forgiveness resides in the Heart, and that it isn't something you do on behalf of the person you want to forgive. Ultimately, forgiveness is about taking our power back from others; it's a totally self-ish thing to do! Many people believe that forgiveness makes right the thing that is being forgiven. But that's not true at all; we forgive for ourselves, not for the other person. Forgiveness sets us free. It's the ultimate payback for whatever anyone has done to us, because until we've forgiven them, they still have power over us.

We can be so full of pride that we don't want to let things go. But if we are going to move forward, we have to forgive. The weight (w-e-i-g-h-t) of what we are holding on to means we will wait (w-a-i-t) even longer for our dreams to come true.

This ties in with one of Caroline's core teachings. According to her, we must release the need to know why things happen as they do. From a logical human perspective, life can seem unfair and chaotic. Yet from a larger, broader perspective— one we cannot fully understand as humans—there is Divine order in all things.

I learned that *Why did this happen to me?* was one of the most toxic questions I could ever ask about life.

I could spend the rest of my life coming up with different answers about why things happened as they did, and never feel fully satisfied.

Through Caroline's work I saw that we are here in "Earth School," and that ultimately the journey of our lives is about *what our soul is learning*, which may in fact be beyond the realm of our human understanding.

Instead of *Why did this happen to me?* I learned to ask, *What am I learning right now?* I've found over and over that the answer to *that* question is far more relevant and satisfying. Why? *Because what you are learning is why it's happening.*

It's all about the lesson, not the circumstance. Learning lessons is much more interesting than spending all your time deconstructing why things happened this way or that way. When I focused on the lesson, I started to *really* take my power back.

Which brings me to the fifth chakra—one of the hardest, perhaps *the* hardest, chakra to master. This energy center is located in your throat, and it's all about how you choose to direct your willpower. Said another way, it's about how you decide to decide.

The mantra for this part of the body is "Surrender your will to Divine will."

Perhaps the most famous fifth-chakra moment in all of human history happened when Jesus was in the Garden of Gethsemane. It's recounted in Matthew 26:37–42 (NIV):

> He took Peter and the two sons of Zebedee along with him, and he began to be sorrowful and troubled. Then he said to them, "My soul is overwhelmed with sorrow to the point of death. Stay here and keep watch with me."

Going a little farther, he fell with his face to the ground and prayed, "My Father, if it is possible, may this cup be taken from me. Yet not as I will, but as You will." Then he returned to his disciples and found them sleeping. "Could you men not keep watch with me for one hour?" he asked Peter. "Watch and pray so that you will not fall into temptation. The spirit is willing, but the body is weak." He went away a second time and prayed, "My Father, if it is not possible for this cup to be taken away unless I drink it, may your will be done."

What a powerful moment and demonstration. *Yet not as I will, but as You will.*

Our world is full of fear. Most of us lack trust that our basic survival needs will be met. Around us we see chaos and violence. Things were no different in Jesus' time, and yet, he was willing to hand over his will to a power greater than himself. Even today, such a prayer can shake us to the core. It's easy to see why this moment in Jesus' life has been referred to as "the Agony in the Garden." Depending on the translation, it is said that Jesus even wept tears of blood, it was such a hard thing to say (Luke 22:44 [NIV]).

People talk about "Christ Consciousness" or "Buddha Consciousness," as if that level of surrender is beautiful and pain-free. But that's not at all true. The prayer "Thy will be done" is perhaps one of the most terrifying sentences any of us will ever say. It takes us out of our own control and into ultimate uncertainty—well beyond what is comfortable for most of us.

The life of Jesus the teacher was not free from anger or pain. In the end it was full of betrayal, torture, and ultimately death. Yet, this is the metaphorical life we have signed up for when we enter into the spiritual path.

The spiritual path, the path of embodying Love, is a humble path. It's a path full of problems, agony, and confusion. It is also a path of joy that can lead to bliss, yes, but not without hardship. For when we surrender our will to the will of the Divine, we are asking for all the things that do not serve God to be removed—which means that all hell may break loose. I don't believe in punishment from God, but I do believe in lessons. As I like to say, *the Uni-verse has shaken you to awaken you.*

But back when I began listening to *Energy Anatomy*, I didn't have this perspective. I recall the very first time I said "Thy will be done"—the words shook me to my core. I curled up on my floor in Los Feliz and cried for about half an hour out of sheer terror. When we make this request, we are asking for the whole of our lives to be uprooted. It's scary and it can hurt. But I've discovered that surrender is short-term pain that pays off in the long run. Because no matter how hard it feels, eventually you come out on the other side—and you'll be in a magical new world you could not possibly have imagined.

If you are worried that surrendering to God's will—or the will of the Divine—won't make you happy, relax. On the deepest level God's will is for you to be happy. It most likely won't look like what you expected, but it will be incredible.

intuition and the heavens: the sixth and seventh chakras

After the fifth chakra comes the sixth chakra, which is located between and slightly above your eyebrows—your "third eye" as it's called in woo-woo land. I like to think of it as your brain. Not surprisingly, this energy center is all about the mind and reasoning. Caroline Myss's mantra for this chakra is "Seek only truth."

I feel like I've lived in this chakra for most of my life. As I said before, having biologist parents meant this center was well developed in me. My mind was very good at convincing me what was true. However I did not know how to seek "Truth" with a capital *T*.

As it turns out, the mind is an incredible tool that allows us to *look for only what we want to see*, and most of the time we find it. This is the "confirmation bias" I mentioned at the start of this chapter. For example, if you believe you are unworthy and not good enough, you will go looking for confirmation of that belief. You'll start to "see" more of that in the world—paying more attention to the cues that support that belief than those (equally or perhaps more prolific cues) that counter it. In other words, the sixth chakra confirms the great spiritual truth "Seek and ye shall find." The question is—what you are seeking?

Once I started studying the sixth chakra, I realized that no matter what I was looking for, I was finding it. For most of my life I was seeking evidence that I wasn't enough—that I didn't matter. I found evidence that I wasn't good enough and because of that I felt I didn't deserve Love and someone like me could never really recover from all the mistakes I had made. *Uh-oh*, I thought. *Better start looking for something else.*

So instead of seeking evidence for my unworthiness, I started to look for proof of my *worthiness*. I started to look for proof of my talents and proof that the Uni-verse was on my side.

The key here is that you can't start looking for the massive outcomes of life first. If you do, you won't take the steps needed to create a small win. Life is all about the small wins; it's all about little steps being taken every day. Big outcomes are the accumulation of many small outcomes. This part of our energy system asks us to celebrate the small wins—which in time will turn into big Truths.

Sixth-chakra work requires us to question beliefs we may have held for a very long time. What's cool about beliefs is that they can change—and so can neural pathways in the brain. Humans used to think the world was flat, that flight was impossible, and that only wooden ships could float. But of course none of those "truths" were actually *true*—even though they seemed to be so. As it turns out, a belief is just a feeling of absolute certainty. Regardless of whether it's correct! When I learned that, I started to question what I believed to see if it was actually true.

Around this time I came across an incredible quote by writer Richard Bach: "Argue for your limitations and you get to keep them." I began to see that *I was the one getting in my own way*. Here I thought the world was limiting me, when in fact *I* was actually limiting me. My beliefs were determining my reality.

Noticing and changing my beliefs is an ongoing practice that I work with to this day.

In fact, it took a revision of my belief system for me to get behind the seventh and final energy center. Because the seventh chakra is about our connection to "The Divine," and the concept of the Divine itself bumped up against a lot of my ideas about reality. But what Caroline taught me with this chakra is that Divinity is much more grounded than I would imagine. No sky gods here.

The best way I can sum up this chakra is to say that the Divine lives in the present moment. To me, the Divine is not some guy in the sky with a beard, but an always-present energy of Love that surrounds and supports all matter, encouraging it to grow and evolve. What's true about the Divine is that it only exists now. We came from Love and when we die we will return to Love. The lesson of the seventh chakra is to let go of the past and do our best not to anticipate the future. Instead, we must bring our mind and our focus to the present. Only then can we begin to truly manage our choices and take our power back.

When I got present, I saw there was so much from the past I was holding on to. (And still am.) It's a lifelong process to let go of the past, and it starts with acceptance. People ask me all the time how to let go, and acceptance is the only answer I can give. First we must accept what happened and not wish it away. The past happened and we can't change it. What we *can* change is what the past *meant*; we can start to see it in a new way. But to try to change anything in the past is futile. Life doesn't work that way.

Similarly, it's impossible to know what's ahead. Yet it's easy to get so paralyzed by our future-tripping that we never take action. For a long time I was really good at staying safe—and stuck. I would go over every possible worst-case scenario, and had a very hard time imagining a future that included anything other than crashing and burning.

It only got worse when I looked back over what had happened in my life to date. Moving to LA with big hopes—and then watching my dream of working at Geffen Records come crashing down. It seemed like a cruel joke—as if God was saying, "Here's a taste of what you want, but you can never have it." Going for my dreams had caused so much pain, I was terrified to try again.

But then I started working with my seventh chakra. As I started to look around I could see that, in the present moment, all my needs were met. I had a roof over my head. I had some food to eat. I had water. I had some gas in my car. The horrible future I was imagining hadn't come true. For me, the lesson of the seventh chakra—which brings together the lessons of the other six—is to bring my awareness to the present time. Here, in this moment, even though I may be terrified of what's to come, everything is as it ought to be.

The work of Caroline Myss was groundbreaking for me. I hope that one day *Energy Anatomy* will be taught in schools, because it teaches simple concepts that change lives. More than anything else, Caroline Myss helped me learn how to take back the power I'd been projecting "out there," and bring it home—to me.

Caroline's guided meditation program *Spiritual Power, Spiritual Practice* is a morning-and-evening meditation that helps you consciously take your power back and "clear your chakras." If you don't like the idea of clearing your chakras—it sounds a little woo, even for me—think of it as a "power scan." You're consciously scanning for where your power is, whose approval you're seeking, and what thoughts are holding you back. Then, you're bringing your power back into your own hands.

There was a six-month period where just about all I did was listen to this meditation, morning and night. One of the key phrases that's still drilled into my mind is *Release the need to know why things happen as they do and bring your attention to the present moment.* That idea is so simple—yet truly profound. Combine it with the idea of surrendering your will to the Divine, and get ready for your life to change dramatically. I know mine did.

One last bit of advice before you begin. As you start down this spiritual path, you've got to be willing to see each moment like a child does: as brand-new. Your perception plays a huge role in changing the story of your life. If you aren't willing to let yourself go back to the beginning, you can't expect to make a clean start to your own hero's journey—which, as it happens, was the lesson I learned next.

— chapter 5 —

FINDING THE THREAD
OF THE HERO'S PATH

Furthermore, we have not even to risk the adventure
alone, for the heroes of all time have gone before us. The
labyrinth is thoroughly known. We have only to follow
the thread of the hero path, and where we had thought
to find an abomination, we shall find a god. And where
we had thought to slay another, we shall slay ourselves.
Where we had thought to travel outward, we will come
to the center of our own existence. And where we had
thought to be alone, we will be with all the world.

—JOSEPH CAMPBELL,
THE POWER OF MYTH

THE ANSWERS TO MY QUESTION—*How can I feel as good off*
the drugs as I do on the drugs?—kept coming. After discovering Caroline Myss and deciding to be open to spirituality again, it was as if all the information I needed started to flood in.

I was still managing bands, but by this point it was financially motivated. What used to be a passion felt like forced labor. I was sick of having my livelihood based on how hard others felt like working. Being a music manager can be a very codependent thing. If the client is happy, you're happy. If the client isn't happy, you aren't happy. And if the client decides not to work or has a drug overdose (or a mood swing, for that matter), it has major ramifications on your life. When I started out it seemed I was built for this lifestyle, but the deeper down the rabbit hole I got, the more I questioned that assumption.

But I couldn't quit, I told myself. I was making a living! What would I do for money if I quit? Surely being spiritual couldn't pay the bills, and even if it could, how? I didn't know the first thing about teaching other people. I was still a messed-up recovering addict and a failure in the music business.

What would I do? I felt lost. Caroline Myss's work had tuned me up and gotten me back on the road, but I felt like I had no map. I understood the concepts of the chakras, but I didn't know what to do with them.

Around that time, I had an intuition to start watching the *Star Wars* movies again. I hadn't watched them since I'd moved to LA, which was a long time for me. But now I was going through an existential crisis, and I had an intuition there was some truth in there that I may have missed as a kid. It was just a hunch—a knowing, a guess. But one night I curled up in my Los Feliz apartment in the Hills, and decided to watch *The Empire Strikes Back*. As any *Star Wars* fan knows, that is the best of them all. I popped in the movie, keen to look for messages; something I might have missed before, that I was supposed to know about life.

It got to the part in the movie where Luke goes to Dagobah, the planet where he is to meet his new Jedi mentor, Yoda (the little green guy). Now I had seen these scenes over three dozen times as a child. Back then, this section seemed boring because there was no action. But this time I saw it with new eyes.

Luke is training with Yoda, and they start discussing the difference between the dark side and the light side of the Force. Luke asks Yoda how he will know the difference, and Yoda tells Luke that he is on the light side when he feels "calm, at peace." Their training wraps up for the day and Luke notices a dark and sinister cave. He says he feels cold and "death" coming from it.

Yoda says that this cave is strong with the dark side—and that Luke must go in. When Luke asks what's in the cave, Yoda responds, "Only what you take with you." Luke starts to put on his weapon belt and Yoda urges Luke to leave them behind. Luke takes one more look at the cave and decides to bring his weapons even though his mentor said he didn't need them.

As Luke descends into the cave, he sees snakes and lizards. It's a tiny passage that finally widens. In a flash he sees his nemesis, Darth Vader, ahead of him. Each draws his lightsaber and they begin to battle. Luke prevails, decapitating Vader. As Vader's head rolls to the ground, the mask blows open to reveal Luke's own face.

When I saw this it made my whole body shiver. It was as if some deep truth was being revealed to me. I paused the movie and looked at Luke's face, buried in the mask of evil, and it hit me: I had to face my deepest fears.

I'm not enough and never will be.

I'm never going to amount to anything.

Who am I to make something of myself?

It'll never get better and it will always be this way.

These very thoughts were the things holding me back. That night, I realized that deep within my own darkest fears were the lessons I needed to learn. I saw that I am not separate from my fears; they are a part of me that *must be faced*.

The question became—how?

Luckily, *Empire* didn't let me down: the answer was just a few scenes away.

Yoda is instructing Luke on how to use the Force. Luke is doing a handstand, and Yoda is standing on Luke's feet in the air. Simultaneously Luke is using the Force to stack rocks. He starts to stand on one hand, and Yoda is impressed. Except just then, R2D2 starts beeping like crazy and Luke loses his concentration. He falls, and so does Yoda.

Luke goes over to see what all the noise is about, and sees that his X-Wing ship has sunk into the swamp. All that's sticking out is its nose.

What happens next changed my life forever. To quote:

Luke: Oh, no. We'll never get it out now.

Yoda (irritated): So certain are you. Always with you it cannot be done. Hear you nothing that I say?

Luke: Master, moving stones around is one thing. This is totally different.

Yoda: No! No different! Only different in your mind. You must unlearn what you have learned.

Luke (tentatively): All right, I'll give it a try.

Yoda: No! Try not. Do. Or do not. There is no try.

Luke closes his eyes and concentrates on thinking the ship out of the swamp. For a moment, the X-Wing's nose begins to rise—but just as quickly it slides back and disappears into the swamp.

Luke: I can't. It's too big.

Yoda: Size matters not. Look at me. Judge me by my size, do you? Hmm?

Luke shakes his head.

Yoda: And well you should not. For my ally is the Force. And a powerful ally it is. Life creates it, makes it grow. Its energy surrounds us and binds us. Luminous beings are we, not this crude matter. You must feel the Force around you. Here, between you, me, the tree, the rock, everywhere! Yes, even between the land and the ship!

Luke: You want the impossible.

Luke then walks away in disbelief, but little Yoda turns toward the swamp and concentrates. He raises his hand toward the sunken ship, and miraculously it begins to emerge. R2 is so freaked out he moves out of the way, and a few moments later the impossible has happened: Luke's previously sunken X-Wing has fully emerged, free from its swampy bondage. Luke stares in astonishment.

Luke: I don't . . . I don't believe it.

Yoda: That is why you fail.

I paused the movie once again. There were shivers down my spine. I couldn't believe it: all this time, such deep wisdom had been buried within my favorite childhood movie!

The words *That is why you fail* were burned into my mind. I couldn't help but think about my current life circumstances. I had "failed" because I wasn't able to face my deepest fears. In the music business, I kept doing drugs instead of feeling my feelings. I couldn't admit when I was wrong.

I didn't have empathy. I didn't know how to forge true relationships, and after a while I thought it was "Hollywood's fault" and not my own. And this is what made me fail. And I was continuing to "fail" because I didn't believe things could be any different. It was a profound moment. A larger world was opening up in front of me: a world of even deeper uncertainty and, yes, even a world of magic and mystery. I had no idea what lay on the other side of this revelation, but I was excited to find out.

it's not about the finger

I tried to watch the *Star Wars* movies again and again in the weeks and months that followed, but a great sadness would come over me every time. After some introspection I realized that I was sick of watching someone else go on a wonderful adventure. *I* wanted to be the hero! I wanted to self-actualize, go on my own adventure, and in turn inspire others to do the same. I didn't know how to get started, so I began researching the creator of *Star Wars*, George Lucas. It's safe to say I was a little obsessed (in a good way).

Around this time I was also going to a lot of therapy with a woman named Trinka Terra. (You can read about her practice at www.katrinkaterra.com.) I was seeing her a couple times a week, to work out what was coming up for me. I felt called to go to therapy because I felt stuck and I needed answers I didn't have and neither did my friends. My mom was really happy for me to go to therapy, but my dad said he thought that therapists were people that you "pay to be your friends." He's a big Beatles fan and so I said, "Sometimes you get by with a little help from your friends." Personally I don't think you find yourself on a therapist's couch because you're "messed up." I believe we all need guides and people to help us work out our existential questions. I felt a deep calling to go to therapy and to learn from Trinka. She had become my Yoda, my version of the oracle in *The Matrix*. Every hero needs a real-life, in-person mentor, and Trinka was mine. I would read books and watch movies and report to her what I was learning.

One day Trinka told me a story about a Zen master. He was smiling with total joy while pointing at the moon in the night sky. Most of his students were confused and sad, seeing only his extended finger and wondering why it was bringing him such joy. But there was one student who was looking past the master's finger, toward the moon. He, too, had a smile on his face.

The moral of the story is that we cannot look to our mentors as our source of power. Instead, we must look where they are looking, and find our own answers.

As usual, the lesson came at the perfect time—right in the middle of my investigation into George Lucas. Up until that point I had definitely been looking *at* him, hoping for answers. Who was this man? What was his story? But after that session with Trinka, I started to look *where he was looking*. Who inspired him? Who were *his* teachers?

I learned about his special relationship with his mentor, Francis Ford Coppola; his friendship with Steven Spielberg (another director whose movies always touched me deeply with their childlike awe); and the time that George and Francis spent working together in San Francisco at American Zoetrope (Coppola's production company). I couldn't believe all these profound filmmakers not only knew each other, but were actually friends! More than that, they had all been inspired by the same man: the great Japanese filmmaker Akira Kurosawa. I started to study Kurosawa's movies and I soon saw how many parallels could be found between *Star Wars* and Kurosawa's work—especially *Seven Samurai*.

As I kept digging into what inspired George Lucas, I saw he had another mentor—a man whose work would become the centerpiece of my life. The man was Joseph Campbell.

While studying film at USC, Lucas had come across the work of Joseph Campbell in an anthropology class. Later, as he was writing *Star Wars,* he was feeling lost in the grand scale of the film. His intention had been to create a myth for a new generation—no small accomplishment. One day he recalled a book he had studied at USC called *The Hero with a Thousand Faces.* In that book, Joseph Campbell reveals a universal pattern found in myths across time and culture. It's a cycle of events he called "the Hero's Journey"—12 steps that are taken by the heroes of almost all great stories ever told. It didn't matter what religion or race or culture, all the great stories share the same basic structure. While the stories of Christ, Buddha, and Arjuna (in the Hindu tradition) look very different, underneath the action they all go through the same birth-death-rebirth cycle of transformation.

At the start of all great stories, the hero is shown in her "ordinary world"—her regular life. But this ordinary world is interrupted by a "call to adventure" in which the hero is invited into some sort of frightening but exciting journey. What follows are tests, trials, and ordeals. The hero meets all kinds of enemies and allies as she progresses toward the greatest trial of all: her own death. And after death she is reborn with new insight, which brings her to the truth of her own heart. With this new understanding the hero once again faces death—and in doing so, saves her family or country from certain destruction. After this heroic deed, she then must share this new insight with her home community. The journey is not complete unless it's shared with others.

Over and over again, the hero must come to terms with her own mortality and death. In doing so, she transcends into a deeper realm—one where magic and dreams come true.

To learn more about the Hero's Journey in depth, go to DailyLove.com/JosephCampbell. I also highly recommend *The Writer's Journey* by Christopher Vogler—he does the best job of breaking down Campbell that I've seen.

Back to my own journey. I discovered that George Lucas had reread *Hero with a Thousand Faces* and used it to create the structure for his mythic film *Star Wars*. The rest is history—*Star Wars* became a megahit. At the time, Lucas very openly gave credit to Campbell for the Hero's Journey structure, and his acknowledgment launched Campbell into the mainstream. From that time onward, screenwriters, poets, musicians, and artists of all kinds have used Campbell's work to help them create universal stories that touch the hearts of millions.

As for me, I became obsessed with studying Joseph Campbell. I saw him as the moon the Zen master was pointing toward. I started to see it wasn't that *Star Wars* itself had so mesmerized me, but the deeper truth that Luke's journey represented.

Campbell used to say that our use of the word *myth* has it all wrong. Many people use the word *myth* as a synonym for *lie*. When we say something is "mythical," we're basically saying it's a figment of someone's imagination. But that's not what the word *myth* really means. Campbell says a myth is a metaphor for *something so big we can't really describe it*. It points us to an experience so enormous it's hard to get our minds around. Myth is the place where the outside world of form meets our own inner eternity. It's a metaphor for God.

Campbell writes,

God is a metaphor for a mystery that absolutely transcends all human categories of thought. . . . I mean it's as simple as that. . . . So half the people in the world are religious people who think that their metaphors are facts. Those are what we call theists. The other half are people who know that the metaphors are not facts and so they're lies. Those are the atheists. (*The Hero's Journey: The World of Joseph Campbell*)

This felt so true to me. I started to understand why I had not fit in at my Christian school: my classmates had taken God literally, while on an intuitive level I knew God was just a metaphor for something bigger than any of us could really comprehend.

"All religions are true," Campbell says, "yet none are literal."

I began to see that, throughout our history, most of humanity has gotten caught up in the semantic names for God (Jesus, Allah, Jehovah, Krishna, and so on) instead of focusing on the essence that those names represent.

Yet again, Trinka's image came to mind—that of the master pointing toward the moon and all but one of his students looking at his finger. What if the essence behind all religions were the same thing, expressed in many different ways? What if we silly humans just got caught up in the names, and forgot the real point—which is Love?

One day soon thereafter I was in my apartment in Los Feliz, contemplating this possibility. I saw the sun outside my apartment window. It dawned on me that from the beginning of mankind, all over the world, all people everywhere saw that very same sun. And yet each culture, race, and geographical area had a different name for that golden orb in the sky:

English = *sun*

French = *soleil*

Hindi = *sÐraja*

German = *sonne*

Ancient Egyptian = *Ra*

How fascinating! The same *essence,* but different *words.* I knew the same was true for God. But it's much easier to talk about the sun, because it's visible and measurable. With something as big as God, it's a lot harder to find words. When it comes to God we are dwelling in the realm of the mystical— the realm of the *mythical.*

The more I learned about the hero's journey, the more I started to see it all around me. I started to understand religion—and all spiritual teachings—as just metaphors bringing me back to my own experience of the Divine mystery.

Finkle Is Einhorn!

In studying Campbell, I came across the work of the great Carl Jung. Jung was the creator of the concept of "archetypes"—symbolic characters, behaviors, or events representing universal human ideas. They are all over storytelling, mythology, and religion. For example, think of what a "master" looks like. What comes to mind? Perhaps a wise old man, such as Yoda? And when I say "Wicked Witch," are you seeing a pointy green nose peeking out from under a black hat? When I say "resurrection," do you see a phoenix rising from the ashes, or maybe Jesus on the cross? These words refer to universal archetypes—symbols familiar to most people. Meaning that upon hearing these words, *most* people would see the same or similar image in their minds.

Then I remembered: Caroline Myss also talks about archetypes! She explains that each of us embodies different archetypes over the course of our lives.

Suddenly I was having a giant cosmic AHA MOMENT! I had been given Caroline Myss's CDs and in my head I classified them as "spirituality and self-help." I had found Joseph Campbell and Carl Jung and classified them as "myth and story." But when you get down to it, they are actually the same thing.

Caroline Myss, it turns out, had studied Carl Jung. All roads lead to Rome, as they say.

The hero's journey is a spiritual journey. It's what all self-help and spiritual material is pointing us toward. In that way, the great stories, movies, and myths are *fictionalized self-help material*—demonstrating through the universal power of archetypes what path we, ourselves, must walk.

I felt like Ace Ventura. *"Finkle is Einhorn. Einhorn is Finkle!"*

It blew my mind and changed my worldview. Everything I had been pursuing in the realm of the mythical was really the experience of honoring my own deep calling.

The key word being *experience.*

We all have knowledge, but what we need in order to transform is *experience*. Suddenly it was crystal clear why it was so hard for me to watch *Star Wars*: I was repeatedly seeing someone else go on their hero's journey, and I was dying to go on *mine*. I had spent the last few years of my life helping my clients achieve their creative dreams, and I had sacrificed my own creativity in the process.

Soon thereafter I came upon one of Joseph Campbell's wisest and most oft-quoted phrases which, when he first spoke it, vibrated throughout the ages: "Follow your bliss."

Yes, this phrase has since become a cheesy ankle tattoo. But it actually speaks to a deep, timeless wisdom. Campbell says the concept comes from the Hindu tradition. In that tradition, the experience of "enlightenment" (*brahman* in Sanskrit) is called *satcitananda*. This word is broken down into three roots:

sat (pronounced "SAHT")

cit (pronounced "CHIT")

ananda (pronounced "ah-NAN-da")

Sat means "truth" or "being," *cit* means "consciousness," and *ananda* means "bliss." Campbell wanted to know what the experience of "enlightenment" was like, so he pondered these three terms. When he thought about *sat*—truth or being—he couldn't quite grasp it. Truth is a relative thing, after all. What is actually true? And how can we know for sure? When he got to *cit*—consciousness—he was stumped once again. What exactly *is* consciousness? How does it operate? Campbell didn't know the answer then any more than we know it today. (I was recently at dinner with Harvard neurosurgeon Dr. Eben Alexander, who explained that to this day we still do not know what general anesthesia does to human consciousness; all we know for sure is that it works—most of the time.) But when Campbell got to *ananda*, or bliss, he relaxed. To quote him:

I don't know whether my consciousness is proper consciousness or not; I don't know whether what I know of my being is my proper being or not; but I do know where my rapture is. So let me hang on to rapture, and that will bring me both my consciousness and my being.

Campbell describes this rapture or bliss as "I always tell my students, go where your body and soul want to go. When you have the feeling, then stay with it, and don't let anyone throw you off."

His assumption was that if you can stay true to your bliss, you will find truth and consciousness, since all three are related. And combined, they lead to the ultimate experience a human can have.

In *The Hero's Journey* he says:

> *I have a firm belief in this now, not only in terms of my own experience, but in knowing about the experiences of other people. When you follow your bliss, and by bliss I mean the deep sense of being in it, and doing what the push is out of your own existence—it may not be fun, but it's your bliss and there's bliss behind pain too.*
>
> *You follow that and doors will open where there were no doors before, where you would not have thought there were going to be doors, and where there wouldn't be a door for anybody else.*

It's our job, according to Campbell, to connect back to our bliss and find what makes us come alive. The world— the whole Uni-verse—actually *suffers* if we don't follow our bliss. That doesn't mean it doesn't take courage. That's why we need mentors. It's why we need friends. We can expect to meet foes and come up against all kinds of threshold guardians—both external and internal. But if we can come to terms with our own (metaphorical) death, we will be reborn to a deeper spiritual life and a richer human existence.

There can be no bliss without facing our deepest fears.

At the same time, bliss shows us who we are. Every seed in the whole world is *like* what it came from. An apple seed is like the apple that it came from. When you plant the apple seed, an apple tree will grow. The same can be said for orange seeds, acorns, or avocados. Never in the history of time has someone planted an apple seed and had it produce an avocado. Why is that? Because the seed is *like* what it came from.

The seed of bliss that is planted within you is the same— it mirrors what created it. That's why doors open when you follow your bliss. You're putting yourself on a mission to do God's will in your life, because *God is bliss*. That doesn't mean it won't be hard and there won't be pain. But all we have to do is follow the thread of the hero path. If Joe Campbell can be trusted—and I personally think he can—what's waiting on the other side is a good life:

> What I think is that a good life is one hero journey after another. Over and over again you are called to the realm of adventure, you are called to new horizons. Each time, there is the same problem: do I dare? And then if you do dare, the dangers are there, and the help also, and the fulfillment or the fiasco. There's always the possibility of a

fiasco. But there's also the possibility of bliss. (*Pathways to Bliss: Mythology and Personal Transformation*)

saying yes to the adventure

My takeaway from Campbell was that, once you really understand what your bliss is and you commit to using it as your compass, everything changes.

I had my road map.

I didn't know what my bliss *was*, but I knew two things: my bliss wasn't my addictions and it wasn't being a music manager. So that's where I started. I decided to change everything—and fast. I was done feeling dried up, and I was done following a paycheck. The second chakra is all about our relationship to money and I had been a slave to my paycheck. I had a weak second chakra, you could say, and it was time to change that.

So I followed my bliss and made a new choice. I fired all my music clients.

It was my first step into the bliss-driven world that Campbell spoke of—my first attempt to *be* Luke Skywalker, instead of just watching him.

One client hung around, though, and together we decided to form a company—a record label that would make uplifting music and eventually become a brand. We just needed to think of a name.

Around that time he and I were traveling from LA to Las Vegas for a Nine Inch Nails show. I was feeling down, so we listened to Caroline Myss audios the whole way. When I got to Vegas, I was still at an emotional bottom. I picked up a pad of paper at Caesars Palace and wrote a love letter to myself.

I wrote down all the things I would no longer tolerate in my life and all the things I would do from now on. I promised myself that I would allow myself to feel good and that it was okay to want to feel good. I wrote that I was worthy of living a better life than I was currently living and I wrote that even though I was so scared of what was to come, I knew in my gut that I would be guided, held, and never alone. When I was done I signed it: Love, Yourself.

I showed the letter to my business partner, and we both decided that we'd just found the name of our company: Love Yourself. What followed was my first lesson in the fact that *we teach what we need to learn*. Because—did I love myself?

No.

Is learning that lesson hard?

You bet.

You won't believe what happened next.

— chapter 6 —

WE TEACH WHAT
WE NEED TO LEARN

*When you are inspired by some great purpose, some
extraordinary project, all your thoughts break their bonds,
your mind transcends limitations, your consciousness
expands in every direction, and you find yourself in a new,
great, and wonderful world. Dormant forces, faculties,
and talents become alive, and you discover yourself to be a
greater person by far than you ever dreamed yourself to be.*

— PATANJALI,
THE MAHABHASYA

ONCE YOU COMMIT TO A PATH AND TAKE ACTION, THINGS
start to change. Said another way, when the Uni-verse knows
you are serious, it starts to move into action right along with
you.

This does not, however, mean that there will not be
pain—and I mean a *lot* of pain. That's what the crisis-to-
Grace cycle is about, after all. And I was starting to feel it.
I wanted so desperately to follow my bliss, and I'd taken the

first steps—firing all my clients and starting a new record label. Yet I still felt like a blind man trying to walk through the streets of New York City; I had no idea which way to turn and I kept bumping into things. Bliss was my new compass, but it seemed to be shrouded in fog. I guess the fog had been there all along, but now I was aware of it. As a former music executive in Hollywood, I was used to hobnobbing with celebs and traveling the world. Now here I was, down on my knees trying to feel my way.

The pain of crisis is a natural part of the waking-up process. There are two kinds of pain that I've seen: the pain of staying asleep, and the pain of waking up. When we stay asleep—or choose not to examine our lives—pain is inevitable. An unexamined life will always bring pain because we'll spend most of our time avoiding that which is uncomfortable. All the while we create more and more discomfort for ourselves because we're not aware of the consequences of our actions. If we choose to wake up, on the other hand, we must face the pain of our wounds. But once we start to see—and then Love—our wounds, once we become aware of how they got there, that pain turns to joy. *Every feeling, fully felt, is joy.*

The pain of staying asleep is a quiet longing for something more. It's a yearning for a deeper connection to life. At first, the pain of staying asleep seems easier than the pain of waking up, because it's more subtle. Until, that is, you get to the end of your life—and you realize you just wasted a whole lot of time. When we don't listen to the wake-up call our yearning eventually turns into skepticism and a closed heart. The pain of staying asleep is a path of choosing short-term pleasure that creates long-term pain.

The pain of staying asleep is the story of all addicts and all those who live unrealized dreams.

Waking up, on the other hand, requires us to embrace short-term pain to create long-term joy. It's the harder path. It's a rare path to follow, because none of us wants to consciously cause ourselves pain. But we must feel pain if we are going to awaken. And I was feeling a lot of it.

So I did what I always do when I'm lost and need help: I prayed. My sincere prayers were, "Thy will be done" and "Show me how to follow my bliss."

There was a long period where no answers came.

I've actually come to believe that while we are in transition from one phase of life to another, we sometimes get lost—on purpose. Sometimes there is a Divine fog placed in our path because *we aren't supposed to know the best step.* We aren't *supposed* to have clarity. We're being taught how to relax control—to stop holding on so tightly.

During this Divine fog, it felt as if all the power I once had was gone. I felt truly powerless for the first time in my life. It's no surprise, then, that one of my addictions showed up again with a fury.

I had been off cocaine for a while, but I was still taking Adderall, which is basically legal speed, and is often prescribed for attention deficit disorder. But even though it's legal, cheap, and socially acceptable, as far as I'm concerned Adderall is just as destructive as cocaine.

I had started using Adderall while I was still in the music business, because I liked that it helped me focus and get things done. But even after I had fired all my clients, I was still on it. I was feeling like shit for taking it, but if I didn't I felt tired and bloated all day long.

As I started down the path of finding my bliss, I felt this deep knowing that I had to come off the Adderall. But I wasn't ready yet. I had been on heavy stimulants for years. Who would or wouldn't I be without it? Without my drug, how would I create? Those questions scared me to death. But I knew I had to face my greatest fears. So a few months after I fired my clients, I decided to stop Adderall cold turkey.

It was rough, and I went through withdrawal for a long time. I had no energy and I slipped into a depression. I quickly transferred my addiction from Adderall to food, and started eating anything and everything in sight. It was a step up, but not one I could sustain for very long. I was praying for help. Thankfully, as happens with the Divine, help arrived.

Thank God for iTunes.

I was looking for more Caroline Myss material on the popular media player when I saw that "Other people who bought Caroline Myss also bought Wayne Dyer." I had never heard of Wayne Dyer, but I was intrigued by the name of his book, *The Power of Intention: Learning to Co-create Your World Your Way.* I liked the sound of that. I didn't know what "co-creation" was, but making my world my way? That sounded good to me. I bought *The Power of Intention* on audio; I'm dyslexic, so it's almost impossible for me to read for any length of time—let alone retain the information.

So I got the audiobook and started listening. And I couldn't stop. I listened, and listened, and listened, and listened.

I hung on every word Wayne read. This book summed up, in a practical way, the new belief system I was forming. I must have listened to this book 20 times that first month. It was just on, all the time. While I was working, while I was showering, when I was in the car.

Wayne's voice was the voice of a loving father. He didn't seem quite as on edge as Caroline. I remember when I heard him say, "You are one of those manifestations. You are a piece of this universal intelligence—a slice of God." It totally blew my mind.

Even after getting familiar with Joseph Campbell's work, I still couldn't get my head around this. How could I, this little tiny person, be a piece of God? That seemed so ridiculous. Impossible. I might even have called it blasphemy. Because growing up it had been drilled into my mind that God is God and I am me. We are separate, and I am a sinner who is barely worthy of God's Love and forgiveness. To go from that mind-set to being a "piece of God" was a leap, to say the least.

But I remembered my Bible and a line from the Book of Luke, Chapter 17 (KJV) that's not quoted often enough in Christian circles:

> And when he was demanded of the Pharisees, when the kingdom of God should come, he answered them and said, The kingdom of God cometh not with observation: Neither shall they say, Lo here! or, lo there! for, behold, the kingdom of God is within you.

So maybe I *was* a part of God. Was it possible that all this time I'd been a fish searching for the very water he was swimming in? Was I already inside of God, and not able to see it?

I wasn't sure, but I was willing to test-drive the theory.

Loving yourself, I had now heard from both Caroline Myss and Wayne Dyer, is required for any transformational process. I was ready to set aside my previous approach—abandoning myself to put the interests of my clients first—in exchange for self-love. The problem was I didn't yet understand the difference between self-love and narcissism. So rather than doing the work to genuinely love and appreciate myself, I adopted a toxic mix of self-centeredness, entitlement, and arrogance—in short, putting myself first in all my affairs. I didn't realize that there is a middle path—a place where self-love and serving others meet. Instead I got on board with "narcissism" and it took me for a ride. I went from thinking God was fully outside of me, to thinking God was fully *within* me. In fact, I started to think that on some level I *was* God, not a piece of God (as we all are).

It was a total ego trip. I didn't have a messianic complex, exactly, but I thought I was more powerful than I had previously imagined. I had stepped into the land of the spiritual egoist—that is to say, someone who has read a bunch of books and learned a new vocabulary—but whose consciousness has not yet changed.

I thought I was special because I could throw around words like *intention, archetypes,* and *chakras.* I started judging others as being "less spiritual" than I. It's true that when you step onto a spiritual path you tend to get a new peer group. But when you judge others as being less than, the joke is on you.

So here's this twentysomething kid in early recovery and fresh off of Adderall who thinks he's a badass spiritual guy because he's read some books. It was a recipe for disaster, and disaster came. And once again in one of its most unfortunate forms: success.

you say you want a revolution?

As I said, my former client John and I had named our new company Love Yourself. I can tell you I didn't love *myself*, but I was the guy who was going to go around and make sure that everyone else loved *themselves*. Since John was a musician and I was a music manager, we decided to put out records. We signed an artist, Emma Burgess, and set about making a demo.

Well, soon the demo turned into a full-fledged album. I pulled all the strings I had and got some amazing musicians to play with her: Mike Garson, David Bowie's piano player; and Josh Freese, the best drummer in the business. Our co-producer was a very well-known guitar player himself, and he pulled some strings of his own (so to speak) and hooked us up with some other incredible musicians.

So here we are—me, John, and this high-profile guitar player—producing a record while trying to nurture Emma into a great artist. Some amazing songs were written in those sessions: "Something That You Do," "Massachusetts," "Big

Break," "Back Seat Queen," "Longway," and a cover of the Outfield's song "Your Love." As I go back and listen to them now, these songs stand the test of time. I am still really proud of what we created.

But the record took longer and longer and longer to make. Each delay meant spending more money. I was dipping into my college fund and my inheritance to make this record—but I was all in. Love Yourself Records was going to be a hit if it killed me.

Plus, I was really enjoying the process. John and I had become the best of friends. We already lived across the street from one another in Los Feliz, and now that we'd started the company it felt like us versus the world. We'd stay up late— me inhaling all the self-help material I could get my hands on, and John perfecting the album. In addition to the record, John and I started designing "Love Yourself" T-shirts. We thought that a merch line might help us make money beyond just selling CDs.

The time came, however, when I ran out of money. So I decided I'd go to bartending school and bartend until the company took off. But I got to class on the first day and hated it. I had never disliked anything more than I disliked bar-tending school. There I was, talking big about following my bliss—while going to school for something I hated.

But I needed the money.

When I came home from my second day of class I prayed for a miracle. I didn't want to make money this way. I could already tell it was going to be soul draining. Plus, the last thing I wanted to do was work in an environment where addiction was rampant, and the LA bar scene is an addiction hotbed.

As Grace would have it, the next day I got a phone call that would change the trajectory of my career. My old friend Brian, an agent at William Morris, was calling to tell me their new client—a band called Gnarls Barkley—was looking for a day-to-day manager. Was I interested?

I didn't know the band—I was "spiritual" now, and had stopped paying attention to pop culture. But a quick Google search revealed that their song "Crazy" was topping the charts. I said yes to meeting their manager, and within a week or so I was hired—no bartending for this guy. My new boss was also into self-help material, and I negotiated enough freedom to still work with Emma Burgess. It seemed like my prayers had been answered.

I was high on life. I had some of my clout back in the music business, but without all the sacrifices. I knew Gnarls Barkley only needed short-term management so there was no risk of getting stuck in this job. It had arrived just to help me pay the bills to get through the next part of my journey. In fact, I was sure the job had been sent by God.

can i be free like the birds? (or this, too, will pass)

The next mind-bending book I discovered was *A New Earth* by Eckhart Tolle. I bought the audio the day it came out and, once again, listened to it over and over. Eckhart became the fourth powerful voice in the chorus of my transformational teachers.

What I learned from Eckhart above all else is that the present moment is all we ever have. I had never really considered that before. As a music manager—and before that, as a dreamer—I was always envisioning some lofty dream or ideal outcome. I loved to look to the future and imagine what was possible.

I was also too scared from the past to live in the present moment. There was so much pain in my past that I couldn't imagine a present moment without pain, so I just tried to avoid it. In fact, I realized I had spent most of my time and money up until that point trying to escape the present.

One day as I was listening to *A New Earth* I saw a pair of birds flying outside of my window. They seemed to be dancing together, without a care in the world. It was as if they were playing for no reason.

I was jealous of the birds in that moment. I wanted to be able to be that present—to just play and be happy for no reason. But that kind of effortless joy seemed so far off. For me, the present moment was loaded down with stress and anxiety.

I didn't know how to get present, but *A New Earth* really helped me take a big step in that direction. One story in particular touched me profoundly:

According to an ancient Sufi story, there lived a king in some Middle Eastern land who was continuously torn between happiness and despondency. The slightest thing would cause him great upset or provoke an intense reaction, and his happiness would quickly turn into disappointment and despair. A time came when the king finally got tired of himself and of life, and he began to seek a way out. He sent for a wise man who lived in his kingdom and who was reputed to be enlightened. When the wise man came, the king said to him, "I want to be like you. Can you give me something that will bring balance, serenity, and wisdom into my life? I will pay any price you ask."

The wise man said, "I may be able to help you. But the price is so great that your entire kingdom would not be sufficient payment for it. Therefore it will be a gift to you if you honor it." The king gave his assurances, and the wise man left.

A few weeks later, he returned and handed the king an ornate box carved in jade. The king opened the box and found a simple gold ring inside. Some letters were inscribed on the ring. The inscription read: This, too, will pass. "What is the meaning of this?" asked the king. The wise man said, "Wear this ring always. Whatever happens, before you call it good or bad, touch this ring and read the inscription. That way you will always be at peace."

I was so moved by this story. "This, too, will pass." I had heard that phrase before, but not in this context. Suddenly I started to see the true impermanence of life. I think most of us assume this phrase is referring to life's bad times—don't despair, this won't last forever. While that is true, I saw the other side of the coin as well. I remember thinking, *Gee, I want to remember this during the good times, too—because those won't last, either.*

This timeless phrase was the exact wisdom I needed to take a step toward being present. It reminded me that even the horribleness I was feeling about the present moment was going to pass; it wasn't always going to be this way. The phrase was so powerful I considered getting it tattooed on my forehead so I'd never forget it.

As it turned out, I didn't need the tattoo. Impermanence was about to take up permanent residence in my life.

learning to live through death

I had very little certainty in my life, but I knew one thing: together, John and I could do anything.

My apartment turned into the editing bay for Emma's record. John was a night owl, so when I would go to bed around 9 or 10 P.M.—after doing my Wayne Dyer "Japa" meditations—he would be in the other room working on the record until the wee hours of the morning.

I would then wake up early and start working on the business side of Love Yourself, just as he was going to sleep. We were a 24-hour team; it seemed like we couldn't be stopped. We were united in our mission to make Love Yourself and Emma Burgess into household names.

But as the wheel of life would have it, John's father was diagnosed with cancer. It was heartbreaking. John's father was his best friend—the man who believed in him more than anyone else, the one who would always push him toward his dreams and cheer him on as those dreams became reality.

With the diagnosis, everything changed. I watched my friend work and work during the day, go home to be with his family in the evenings, and come home late feeling beaten.

As time went on, it became more and more obvious that his father was becoming terminal. As we got closer to the end, I was there for John. His father was in a hospital way out of town, and I told him that when the time came I would be there to drive him to the hospital to say good-bye. Early one morning, I got a hysterical call from John. Today was the day.

I rushed out of bed, threw some clothes on, picked John up, and we sped off. When we had 40 or 50 miles left to go, I floored it. It was about 6 A.M., and I must have been going 100 miles an hour or more. I didn't care if the SWAT team and the Marines came after me; I was getting my friend to that hospital in time. I decided it was worth facing the consequences to ensure that my friend got there before his father passed.

After what felt like an impossibly long ride, we arrived. When we got into the ICU, it wasn't a good scene. John's family was there and his father was hooked up to machines and looking pretty bad. I tried my best to move into a Loving space, but I'd never been in a situation like that before. I wasn't quite sure what to do. I just held space, knowing that my friend's father could go at any time. We all held hands, gathered around, and whispered Loving things into his ear to let him know that he was Loved and not alone. After a little while, he was gone.

It was a tragic moment that I was not ready for. The experience was so intense that I went into shock; I was not able to feel my feelings. I did my best to "stay present," as I was learning from Eckhart, and it was the practice of being present that allowed me to witness a miracle in that very room.

I had never seen someone die before, and I was mesmerized. I watched his body for about five or ten minutes after he passed. I couldn't take my eyes off of him. I remember there was a very distinct moment when he went from being a living being to simply a body. I saw it change form—it was as if his Spirit had just left. I was able to see the transition happen. I cannot describe it other than to say I saw his Spirit leave, and after that, he was no longer a human being. His body was just the leftover container. It was one of the most spiritual, transcendental, out-of-my-mind experiences of my life. It was the closest to God and the Divine that I've ever witnessed. Nothing, and I really mean *nothing*, even comes close.

After a lot of reflection, I now understand that experience to have been one of the pivotal moments of my life. It changed me for good, forever. Face-to-face with death, I found myself motivated and inspired about life. I understood two profound truths. The first was that life is beyond precious. There are no words to describe how important and Loved each and every one of us is. At the same time, we are fragile and can be gone in a moment. There are no guarantees. I'd heard that said plenty of times before, but that night it became more than some trite cliché. I knew it at the depths of my Soul.

In getting off Adderall, I had seen some lows. For a while I even felt suicidal. But after witnessing this death, I decided

I would rather face my fears than die a coward. That meant suicide was out. What was ahead was unknown. While I didn't know it at the time, watching my best friend's father pass had prepared me for the next leg of my journey. Having had that experience, there was nothing that could stop me from giving my gift to the world.

If I hadn't gone with John that morning, I can honestly say there would be no *Daily Love*. I would have been too afraid to begin. I would have turned back and chickened out. That experience didn't make me fearless, but it did give me the courage and perspective I needed to fully understand that when fear arises, we have to choose to face it, instead of living a life of regret.

Soon after the death came the funeral. John and I took it upon ourselves to bury his father, shoveling the dirt on top of his grave. I had never been so close to death, and had never been so close to someone who had lost their best friend. The following week I got "This too will pass" tattooed on my right arm in honor of John's father. I decided I wanted to live like I was dying from that moment onward.

these t-shirts will change your life

Shortly thereafter, John and I had a meeting with Emma Burgess and her attorney. She told us she didn't like the record we had made and was moving on. Within just a couple of weeks John had lost his father and we had lost our artist. What were we to do?

God was keeping me afloat. I had recently stopped working for Gnarls Barkley and, after a quick four-month stint as Hugh Jackman's assistant, I had taken a job as senior VP of a new music management company.

I'd negotiated a deal with the company, which meant I could still work on Love Yourself. While we waited for another music artist to come along, John and I decided to redouble our efforts on the merch line. We decided to spend the money we had left on T-shirt production—something neither of us had ever done. It was exciting—we decided we were going to bring self-love to the masses through apparel. We wanted to mix hip graphics with spirituality and make consciousness cool.

So we designed a handful of T-shirts. For a while, nothing happened. Then I discovered my boss's wife was a fashion buyer for a large retail store. We showed her our samples, and she loved them. She taught us the basics of the fashion business and then she introduced us to a showroom. A showroom is a place where fashion designers display their products, and store buyers come to see a lot of clothes at once. Getting into a showroom means you're more likely to sell your clothing into large accounts.

We got into a showroom in downtown LA just in time for a thing called the "LA Market," which is when stores from all over the world come to LA to see the new trends. To our surprise, our T-shirts sold! We even got picked up by the prestigious Lisa Kline store on Robertson Boulevard. I was sure we were the new fashion gurus of self-love, appointed by God to teach the masses about Loving themselves.

The pressure was on. We had the orders; now we needed to make the T-shirts. We went all over LA trying to find a vendor who could deliver a small order on our schedule. We eventually found one who made the T-shirts, but they barely delivered them on time.

Because of the success of the LA Market, we were able to get into one of the top fashion trade shows in the world. It was called Project, and it was coming up soon. We had to develop a bigger line of products with more stuff to sell—fast. So we busted our butts and created a full line of T-shirts and samples.

We were up all day and night making it happen.

We got to Project and the best thing in the world (which would again prove to be the worst thing in the world) happened: we got a $60,000 order from the Japanese division of Kitson, an upmarket LA department store. All in all, we ended up writing about $100,000 in orders at Project. A few weeks later Lehman Brothers crashed and the Great Recession started, but John and I were rolling in dough.

Kind of.

You see, when you sell $100,000 in T-shirts, that means you have to come up with about $40,000 to *make* the T-shirts. We didn't have the cash. I placed the order with the manufacturer anyway, and full-on applied the power of intention to manifest the money. We begged, borrowed, and stole—and eventually made it happen.

It was the effort of a lifetime, but we produced all those darn shirts and actually got them shipped.

As you can imagine, I now thought I was the shit. I'd made more money in a single trade show than in a whole year in the music business. I was impressed with myself, and addicted to the rush of success. We started to expand—fast. I hadn't yet heard the business adage "Grow . . . grow . . . die." I assumed the money would keep coming in. In truth, I had no idea how to spend, save, or invest money to keep a business going.

As we started to grow, John and I discovered we had very different visions of where we wanted the company to go. John wanted to stay small and grow slowly and I wanted to go big and global *now*. We were at odds, fighting a lot. From my vantage point today I can see that it would have been better for the business to grow more slowly, and my impatience played a big role in the demise of the company. Unfortunately, our friendship started to decline along with the business.

Soon I relapsed on Adderall to handle all the stress. It was the icing on the cake—I turned into a total monster. Within a few months, Love Yourself went under.

Looking back I see I had taken it upon myself to teach self-love to the masses because my ego wanted to feel important. But I hadn't really done the work. By "work," I mean the *inner* work. I had gone out into the world with a message that I had not yet embodied. I was like Icarus, flying too high, my wings about to fail me. I had great "intentions," but I didn't yet realize that the spiritual path was not there to make me feel special and good about myself.

I was doing it all wrong.

While at the time it was devastating, today it's obvious to me why Love Yourself crumbled. I was preaching what I, myself, had not yet been willing to learn. I needed to learn humility, first and foremost. And I also needed to discover that I was creative, and that I didn't need to hide behind Emma Burgess or John or anyone else. In short, Love Yourself failed because I hadn't yet learned the next lesson on my journey: what it really meant to trust myself.

— chapter 7 —

THE DIVINE STORM

You can be mad as a mad dog at the way things went. You can swear, and curse the fates, but when it comes to the end, you have to let go.

—THE CURIOUS CASE OF BENJAMIN BUTTON, 2008

KUNDALINI YOGA CAME INTO MY LIFE AROUND THIS TIME.

When I first heard about Kundalini I thought it must be an Italian form of yoga. It sounds like a pasta dish, doesn't it? I can see it now: Kundalini Alfredo—white sauce, noodles, and lentils—a good combination of Italy and India.

Once I actually started practicing Kundalini I thought it should be called "Kunda-looney," because it can only be described as a very *strange* form of yoga. It's not the vinyasa that comes to mind when most of us think about yoga, with all the downward dogs and pigeon poses. It's a breath-based practice that helps you feel better through releasing emotions. It's awesome for anxiety—way better for you than Xanax. Plus if you do it right, the morning after a Kundalini yoga class you will have a *positive* hangover!

As pressure to keep my company going and growing rose—and tensions with John got to their boiling point—there was only one place I could find true solace: my yoga mat. I found myself escaping to Golden Bridge, the local Kundalini studio, during working hours. There, on my mat, I would break down again and again.

At one point I was doing two or three Kundalini classes a *day*. It seemed to counter my anxiety and fear, and made the arguments John and I were having more bearable.

I'd have a fight with John, and hit the yoga mat. I'd review our bills, and hit the yoga mat. I would ask a girl out and get rejected (again), and hit the yoga mat.

It was as if Kundalini yoga was my new teacher. I was doing it as if my life depended on it.

Then one day, in the middle of the downfall of my business, while sitting on a couch in the lobby at Golden Bridge, I suddenly had the idea for *The Daily Love*.

I had been sharing wisdom quotes on social media for years—first MySpace (yes, *that* long ago) and later on Facebook. My favorite website at the time was DailyCandy, which is a hip and cool daily e-mail newsletter about all things fancy and feminine. I thought it would be fun to start a website like DailyCandy, but based on the principles I was learning from Caroline Myss, Wayne Dyer, Joseph Campbell, and others. The URL www.DailyLove.com was already taken (it would take me five years to get it), but TheDailyLove.com was available. So I bought that.

And had no idea what to do with it.

The more Kundalini yoga I did, though, the more I knew

I needed to be writing and not putting energy into a clothing company. This was a hard realization. I had thrown all of my college money, a lot of my parents' money, a lot of John's parents' money, and a lot of time into this project. Taking care of myself—which at the time meant doing Kundalini yoga and writing—meant abandoning all of that. But it was also when I started to *live* the message I'd been preaching—Love Yourself.

It was then that I came up with one of my favorite *Daily Love* tweets ever:

Never abandon yourself to please another.

The "another" in particular I was most worried about at this point was John. And the thought of abandoning him after everything we'd been through was a hard one for me to swallow. It was obvious that our business relationship was in a downward spiral, and was taking our friendship with it. But I was in denial at the time. Buying the Daily Love domain started a phase in my life when I seemed to be allergic to money. It would just run away from me. Our bills were piling up at Love Yourself, and our search for an investor to "save" the company was failing.

One prospective investor gave me the feedback that I needed to "suffer more" before I would be successful. I didn't understand what she meant at the time. But looking back I see she meant that I was in a partnership with someone who wasn't right—and I couldn't see it. I had spent a lot of time with this person and she had gotten to know me well. She was an amazing change agent in my life because she introduced me to SLAA (Sex & Love Addicts Anonymous—man, Love addiction is a biatch) but always was interested in investing in my business. She was right; I needed to suffer more. I had to go through the pain of finding that out for myself.

As things got worse, I got more and more spiritually focused.

I asked my Kundalini yoga teacher, Tej, whether there were Kundalini meditations for abundance. The meditation she gave me was based on the seed syllable *Har* (pronounced "hud"). You chant *Har* for 20 to 30 minutes each day, with your eyes closed. You cup your hands and then hit the top and bottom sides of your hands together. Each time your hands hit, you say *Har*. I did 30 minutes in the morning and 30 minutes at night. All the while I visualized us getting investors, restoring our business partnership and friendship—all the success that Love Yourself *could* be.

But the more I meditated, the worse things got—worse and worse and worse. Our sales team in New York dropped us. Sales from stores dried up. We weren't getting reorders, and pretty soon we were at a standstill. In a last-ditch effort to finance the company and meet our production orders, I made a licensing deal with a company called Band Merch. John didn't think it was a good deal, but I put it through anyway—it was a unilateral decision on my part and it was the nail in the coffin for our relationship. In retrospect I see how impatient I was being, but at the time I was in such a panic I didn't know what else to do.

John was our lead graphic designer, but our partnership was at such an impasse that no new designs were getting done. So I decided I would take our designs and work with the Band Merch design staff to innovate the line. But John wouldn't hand over the design files. As it turned out, we'd never signed a contract that stated the company "Love Yourself, LLC" actually owned John's designs, so he was not contractually obligated to release them.

Without any designs and no new product, Love Yourself was effectively dead.

I kept meditating for abundance, but abundance never came. What happened next I've come to call my "Divine Storm."

what the heck is a divine storm, anyway?

Before I tell you about my Divine Storm, I want to define the term. A Divine Storm is a period of time (it could be a day, a week, a month, a year, or an era) where it literally seems like the whole world—the entire Uni-verse and even God—is against you. It's a time when everything falls apart and there seems to be no way out. It's a time of massive pain. Ultimately, Divine Storms come to clear out whatever is not a part of your next layer of growth. But depending on how stubborn you are, they can shake you pretty bad.

Enter another one of my favorite *TDL* tweets:

The Uni-verse has shaken you to awaken you.

The Divine doesn't act according to your own desires or expectations. The Divine knows you better than you know yourself. It sweeps in to clean the slate, to force you to give up what you have not been willing to surrender. In other words, when you utter the phrase "Thy will be done," expect all hell to break loose.

My Divine Storm was upon me. I thought things were already as bad as they could get—I was losing my business, I had lost my best friend, and I was back on Adderall. But I didn't know the half of it. What was coming next would test every shred of faith I had in myself and in the Divine.

Everything I had come to Love in this new "spiritual" phase of my life was being taken from me. It felt like God was pulling the rug out from under me, for no reason. The following events all happened over the course of *one week:*

- The Buddhist girl I was dating broke up with me.
- John and I ended our business relationship.
- Love Yourself died.
- My roommate told me he was moving out in 30 days.
- Our initial investors in Love Yourself told us that they had lost 70 percent of their wealth in the stock crash and recession.
- My lower back went out.
- I got gout (yes, gout) in my left big toe.

It was one of the worst weeks I'd ever had. Worse than all those years ago when I was on coke and drinking all the time and got fired by Geffen. Because Love Yourself wasn't just a clothing company to me. *It was who I was.* It was my identity, and not just my identity, but also my mission. It was the way I thought I was going to inspire the world and change the course of many people's lives.

In a matter of weeks, Love Yourself was gone. And everything else was gone, too. I had no business, no girl, almost no money, and no place to live. The only things I had were a lot of debt and a gout boot. (Try walking around LA wearing a geriatric ski boot and see how good you feel about yourself.)

I was spending more and more time at my hangout, Golden Bridge Yoga, even with the gout. That week I ran into the owner of Golden Bridge, a woman named Gurmukh. She told me that, according to Louise Hay, gout was all about the need for control. But what could I possibly be trying to control—except a life that was falling apart at the seams?

I was in a full-on crisis and it was really scary. It felt like God and the whole Uni-verse were against me. So I quit the Adderall (for good this time), loaded up my Caroline Myss *Spiritual Power, Spiritual Practice* meditations, kept doing the Abundance Meditations, and hit the Kundalini yoga even harder.

One day while listening to Caroline, I had a momentary glimpse of an idea. *What if this isn't happening* to *you; what if this is happening* for *you?* I don't remember where I had read it, but I remembered her saying that your job is to say your prayer—and then see everything that happens after that prayer as an answer to that prayer.

So, what if my Divine Storm was an answer to my deepest prayer? What if my life crumbling around me wasn't a punishment, but an act of pure Love?

Could that *actually* be true? It seemed crazy to think so. I felt so lost, so abandoned, so alone. I just wanted to turn back. But a glimmer of hope had been sparked.

there's no turning back now

I thought about calling my friends in the music business and trying to go back. It seemed like it would be so easy. Many high-profile agents and managers were just one call away.

But even with everything that had happened, I was still stubbornly clinging to the idea of finding my bliss. It felt like if I went back, I would be abandoning that dream. A deeper part of me knew that for me, the music business meant nothing but pain, addiction, and lack of fulfillment.

There seemed to be only one logical solution: step forward into the scary unknown.

I had been sending out quotes via *The Daily Love* a couple times a week at that point. I looked at my numbers on e-mail and Twitter, and to my surprise I had a thousand followers on Twitter and a thousand e-mail addresses. It was WAY bigger than the Love Yourself database. It seemed that sending out all those quotes and tweeting inspirational musings was . . . *working*. I wondered, *What would happen if I went all in on* The Daily Love? I thought about one of my favorite Will Smith quotes, which I still try to apply to this day: "There's no reason to have a plan B because it distracts from plan A." It was time, yet again, to make a choice with an uncertain outcome—to leap into the unknown. It was time, because I had nowhere else to go.

It was clear that a dramatic downsizing was on the way. When I moved out of my apartment, I gave away most of my furniture and got a small storage unit for the rest. As I considered where I was going to live, I thought about my ex-girlfriend's parents. They were a lesbian couple who lived in the San Fernando Valley, and they were like family to me. Even though I was no longer dating their daughter, we'd stayed in touch. I recalled that they had kindly offered that I could stay in their pool house if things ever got bad. At the time they'd said it, it seemed hard to imagine. But now I was homeless, and I only had enough money in the bank to last three months, tops. The pool house would mean free rent until I could figure out what I was going to do next.

I moved in August 1st, 2009. I planned to stay one month.

The pool house was one eight-foot-square room—the only thing that fit was my bed—with a small bathroom and an even smaller closet. There was no Internet service and here I was trying to start an Internet company. But it was a roof over my head. I put the pedal to the metal, tweeting and e-mailing my butt off. *The Daily Love* became my new obsession. It felt like I was writing for my life. I didn't know if it was going to work, but Will Smith wouldn't let me focus on Plan B, so I didn't have a choice. I think of it as my "Agony in the Garden" moment—that moment when you say "Thy will be done" and you surrender. You literally surrender the outcome to God.

I gave myself a $17-a-day food budget and ate only stuff from Trader Joe's, one of the rare places in LA where you can get a whole day's food for under $17. And my new office was Golden Bridge Yoga. I couldn't afford yoga classes anymore, but my dear friend and teacher Sat Siri let me come to her class for free.

My life became writing, spending as little money as possible, and doing Kundalini yoga. It was the sweet, terrifying place of total surrender.

I remember one day taking a walk in the valley and seeing so many homes filled with families, children—people who had "made it" in my mind. I had never felt so far away from God in my life. Would I ever "get there"? It seemed impossible. It felt like the whole world was going on without me and I didn't matter. I felt abandoned and alone. It was then that I wrote this prayer:

My dear Source of all Creation,
Pick me up when I can walk no further
Help shine a light in this dark place
So I can see just one more step in front of me
Oh heavenly Source please show me the way
When I am lost
For your presence, it comforts me
It restores me to fullness
My Father, My Mother Source
I throw myself at your knees
And bow to your Infinite Wisdom
I know all things are done through me
By you
I am your humble servant

Take me, shake me Oh Muse
To the bone
Make me so scared of you
Yet give me the strength to stand tall
And see that my fear was wrong all along
Shake me to my core
So that I might know what my heart
Really feels like
Strip away everything that is not needed
So that I can see You clearly
In the space that's in between
My Muse, my sweet Muse
Protect me from Death
Until it is my time to move on to greater pastures
Take me to the edge and keep me there
So that I might have one foot in Death
And one in Life
So I can bring these two worlds closer together
Thank you Oh Muse for these
Lessons, these moments of joy and sadness
I know they are your perfect
Recipe
For Bliss

I meant what I said in that prayer, too: I *wanted* to live on the edge. I just didn't want to go *over* it.

I had been in the pool house for about a month. One night I came home after another bad date and borrowed Internet from some poor unsuspecting house in the neighborhood

(I'd sit outside in my Jeep and scan for open Wi-Fi networks) and saw that my e-mail in-box was full to the brim with Twitter notifications. I also looked at my Twitter account and my number of followers had gone up—a lot. In fact, I'd gone from one thousand to ten thousand people overnight. I couldn't believe it. What had happened? Then I saw it: reality TV star Kim Kardashian had tweeted about me. She said, "I feel so inspired when I read tweets from @TheDailyLove. They make me feel lovey and positive!"

I had just gotten another Godshot.

This was a very powerful moment. Suddenly, at the push of a button, I had access to ten thousand people. What was I going to say? Would it be good? I didn't know, but I kept on tweeting. I continued to gain followers, and now people were tweeting back that I was changing their lives with my writing. I couldn't believe that a tweet could change a life, but apparently something was happening. I had a new burst of passion and energy to keep going.

But even as I was being fueled by this wave, I remember looking around the pool house and wondering, *How am I here?* It was so small. It felt like a prison cell. In one of my meditations I asked the question, *Why a room this size? You are so abundant—why something so small?*

The answer I got back was immediate: *Mastin, this room represents the size of your faith.*

The thought gave me chills because I knew it was true. I had surrendered my faith to so many other people. I hadn't followed my true calling, and this room represented how much faith I had in myself—and in God to support me in following my bliss. As I kept meditating, I remembered my Bible and what Jesus said:

> Assuredly I say to you, if you have faith as a mustard seed, you will say to this mountain, "Move from here to there," and it will move; and nothing will be impossible for you. (Matthew 17:20 [NKJV])

I started to laugh out loud. I couldn't believe this! I could probably fit a *billion* mustard seeds in my pool house. I saw that even though I was in such a small room, I was being supported and in fact I had PLENTY of faith. It was in that moment that I began to see that the pool house wasn't my jail, it was my cocoon. I was transforming from a caterpillar to a butterfly, but I had to "die" first.

hurry up and die

There's a moment in every story where the hero must die in order to be reborn. Joseph Campbell calls it "The Ordeal." In *The Hero with a Thousand Faces*, Campbell says: "The ordeal is a deepening of the problem of the first threshold and the question is still in balance: Can the ego put itself to death?"

I knew that this moment of darkness wouldn't last forever. I knew that I was just going through a death, and that rebirth was on the way. I didn't know when or how, but I knew it was coming. What I had to do was trust, which is one of the hardest things. I mean, to lean in on your dreams with all of your faith. The voices of the outside world ask you to seek comfort and financial security. But your comfort zone is not where your dreams reside.

After living with my ex-girlfriend's parents for about three months, people close to me started to get worried. Namely, *my* parents. I've written about how much I love them, and how much they have supported me. They sacrificed a lot of time and money to support my dream of Love Yourself. They were with me all the way. But given how that venture had gone, and now seeing their son in such a strange state, they really started to question my decision to pursue *The Daily Love*.

I don't think it's weird for parents to question their children, to want financial security for them. But I also think that when you are called into the strange abyss of the unknown, you must cast off the fear of survival and approval so that you can enter the land of your dreams.

I am a total mama's boy. For all the years I've lived in LA, not a day has passed when I haven't talked to my mom. During this very hard time in my life, the conversation was generally about my survival—what my next move was going to be. I had come to Hollywood and made it, lost it, gotten clean, started a new company, put my all into it and watched it fail.

Now I was tweeting from a pool house. I might have had ten thousand followers, but I wasn't making money.

It didn't make sense from the outside, and yet I knew it was what I had to do.

My parents kept asking me what I was going to do for money, and when I was going to get a job. Each time they asked, I felt a lot of pain. It was hard enough feeling my way down an unknown path with no idea where I was going. But to have my parents, who I loved so much, asking me when I was going to get a job—it was just too much. I wanted to tell them that I already *had* a job. Tweeting was my job.

It was October 2009. The initial high of the Kim Kardashian tweet had worn off and I felt like I was wandering in a forgotten wasteland of faith. Then, thankfully, help came—in the form of a movie. I find a lot of peace and solace in film; movies are my happy place. I had saved up a lot of ArcLight Cinemas points from back when I had money—thousands and thousands of them—and these points allowed me to see films I wouldn't otherwise have been able to afford.

The movie I saw that day was *Amelia*, the true story of Amelia Earhart. I was so touched by her courage and her desire to fly. As the movie was ending and we see the final shot—Amelia flying off to her death—these words came across the screen:

All the things I've never said for so very long, look up, they're in my eyes. Everyone has oceans to fly, as long as you have the heart to do it. Is it reckless? Maybe. But what do dreams know of boundaries?

That was it! What do dreams know of boundaries?

That was me. Those were the words I had been searching for—the words that described what I was feeling about my dream of creating *The Daily Love*. The next day I called my mother and read her the quote. I said, "If you want to know who your son has become, remember these words."

I told her that I loved her sooo much, and that she meant the world to me. But, I told her, getting a job wasn't in the cards for me. I told her I would rather live on the beach in Venice, CA with my laptop and *The Daily Love* than work a corporate job for six figures.

I just couldn't do it. My soul had to be free.

We never discussed me getting a job again. It was a hard conversation to have, but one worth having. My honesty helped me and my parents come closer together than ever before.

And after making this declaration, things really started to get interesting.

Turns out the William Hutchison Murray quote is true:

Concerning all acts of initiative and creation there is one elementary truth . . . that the moment one definitely commits oneself then providence moves too. All sorts of things occur to help one that would never otherwise have occurred.

love born from anger

After some consideration, I decided to go back to John one more time and tell him that I was moving on from Love Yourself, 100 percent. (I secretly hoped he would say he was sorry, and that maybe we could work things out.) We went to dinner, and I told him "I'm going to do this Daily Love thing.

I want it to be huge. You can be a part of it—we can do it together, with Love Yourself. Let's make this right."

But it was too far gone. He wanted nothing to do with *TDL*, and he was still holding on to the designs. I told him that he was screwing me, the company, and my parents over by not giving us the designs that we paid for. His response, which I'll never forget, was, "I'm a Scorpio, screwing people over is in my nature."

Red-hot anger shot through my whole body. I couldn't believe he was sabotaging our company and blaming it on his astrological sign.

All the hidden anger I had toward myself rose up and got projected onto John. It was overwhelming. I wanted to scream, but instead I decided to go for a jog around the Silver Lake Reservoir. During the run, I decided that it was officially over. I wasn't going back to John or Love Yourself, and I was going to make the *Daily Love* blog the *Huffington Post* of the personal-growth space. There was no going back; as of that moment a line in the sand had been drawn.

While on the run, I saw what *The Daily Love* would become. I saw all the people it would touch and all the good it could do. I saw millions of people reading it. I'll admit I wanted to create something so big John wouldn't be able to ignore it. I thought success would be the best revenge. When I finished the run, I was still angry, but I was also energized. I decided to use my anger toward making something beautiful.

When I got back to my car, I also had a text from a long-time friend—Brian. He wanted to do sushi dinner in Venice, so I went across town to see him. That night, he told me that his company, Cause Cast, was partnering with *The Huffington Post*. He was going to be running the HuffPo's "Impact" section—the section for nonprofits.

I couldn't believe it. Just an hour prior I had set a strong intention to become "the *Huffington Post* of personal growth." And next I discover that my good friend has just become a top editor at the site! If this wasn't yet another confirmation that I was on the right path, I didn't know what was.

A month or so later, I was at the Cause Cast holiday party. It was a mixture of LA political types, activists, and some corporate folks. I wasn't having all that much fun, if I'm honest. That is, until I saw a woman joyfully dancing with two young men.

She was the life of the party and I wanted to know her. So I went up and introduced myself.

"Hi," I said. "My name is Mastin."

"Ashton?" she said. She must have thought I was Ashton Kutcher—we do bear a resemblance (LOL).

"*Mastin*," I said.

"Hi, Mastin, I'm Agapi. Would you like to dance?" She said it with a Greek passion that was contagious. We danced and talked the rest of the night. She gave me her card, and asked me to call her so we could discuss ways we might help each other.

When I called the following week, she invited me to her house for a meeting. I must admit I was surprised by its size (huge) and its location (Westwood). Agapi came to the door and warmly invited me in, asking me to sit in the office while she finished up some things. As I sat there, I looked around and noticed a picture of Agapi and Arianna Huffington. Then I saw a picture of Agapi with Arianna's daughters.

Then I noticed a picture of Arianna Huffington with President Obama. Suddenly I put it together: I was in *Arianna Huffington's office.* Agapi was her sister.

Less than one month after making the declaration that I wanted to be "the *Huffington Post* of personal growth," I found myself literally sitting in Arianna's office chair. At this moment I knew I was never going back to the music business or my old way of life. Dawn was breaking.

That day I saw, many times, that the answer to our deepest prayers means *not* getting what we want. I had surrendered to my Divine Storm, put my trust in God, and let the chips fall where they may, and they'd landed me exactly where I needed to be.

are you Babbitt?

There's a story I love from Joseph Campbell, about what happens if you don't surrender to your bliss. It's from his book *The Power of Myth,* and Campbell is using Sinclair Lewis's novel *Babbitt* as an example:

> *Remember the last line? "I have never done the thing that I wanted to in all my life." That is a man who never followed his bliss.*
>
> *Well, I actually heard that line when I was teaching at Sarah Lawrence. Before I was married, I used to eat out in the restaurants of town for my lunch and dinners. Thursday night was the maid's night off in Bronxville,*

so that many of the families were out in restaurants.

One fine evening, I was in my favorite restaurant there, and at the next table there was a father, a mother, and a scrawny boy about twelve years old. The father said to the boy, "Drink your tomato juice."

And the boy said, "I don't want to."

Then the father, with a louder voice, said, "Drink your tomato juice."

And the mother said, "Don't make him do what he doesn't want to do."

The father looked at her and said, "He can't go through life doing what he wants to do. If he does only what he wants to do, he'll be dead. Look at me. I've never done a thing I wanted to in all my life."

And I thought, "My God, there's Babbitt incarnate."

That's the man who never followed his bliss.

You may have a success in life, but then just think of it—what kind of life was it? What good was it—you've never done the thing you wanted to do in all your life. I always tell my students, go where your body and soul want to go. When you have the feeling, then stay with it, and don't let anyone throw you off.

In order not to end up like Babbitt and to really live your bliss, you must go through short-term pain. The lesson here is that if you don't, you will live the rest of your life unrealized. Be willing to live a few years how most people won't, so that you can live the rest of your life how most people can't.

— chapter 8 —

THE LA MOMS

The glory of friendship is not the outstretched hand, nor the kindly smile nor the joy of companionship; it is the spiritual inspiration that comes to one when he discovers that someone else believes in him and is willing to trust him.

— OFTEN ATTRIBUTED TO
RALPH WALDO EMERSON

Looking back on my journey, and seeing how much help and support I received to get where I am today, I've come to believe that there's no such thing as a "self-made" person. Sure, we can create a life of our dreams with effort, but never by ourselves.

I think of my life as "before Agapi" and "after Agapi."

Agapi Stassinopoulos is one of the most open, loving, and giving people I've ever met. She truly lives a wholehearted life. Without her generosity, love, and compassion, *The Daily Love* would not be what it is today.

And yet it's almost amazing how, with each burst of help I got, there was also an opportunity for me to give back. Agapi took me under her wing and helped me out, but she also needed help. I had become a tweeting and e-mailing master, and she needed to get set up with social media and e-mail marketing.

I also suggested she write a book, and publish it with Hay House. Neither of us had contacts at Hay House, but I suggested she write it and trust that Hay House would publish the book. She started writing, and a month later she got an agent. The agent took the book to Hay House and they bought it! The book, *Unbinding the Heart,* is a loving dose of Greek wisdom from Agapi.

At the same time, Agapi had my back. Literally—I was having lower back problems and she sent me to her chiropractor and paid for it. But she also helped with the business. One day we were meeting and she asked me what I really needed. It was January 2010, and my bank account was going to be empty on March 1st. I had two months to generate revenue. So I told her what I really needed were advertisers for TheDailyLove.com. She thought about it for a moment, and then suggested I meet a man named Tommy Rosen. She told me Tommy was well connected in the yoga world and that he knew lots of conscious companies who might want to advertise.

I will never forget meeting Tommy Rosen for the first time. The man exudes joy. He had a huge smile on his face, and he greeted me with a hug. From the moment I met Tommy I felt like he was my brother. Tommy lives to help other people. He and I would meet, talk about yoga, life, *The Daily Love,* and how he could help me. When Tommy heard

I was down-and-out, he made helping me a priority. I had never met a man so giving.

He definitely knew some potential advertisers, so we worked out a deal where he became my ad sales rep, receiving 15 percent of whatever he brought in. I had never been so nervous—the financial cliff was coming and I needed a miracle. On February 27th, 2010—just a day before I was going to be penniless—I got my first advertising check from a company called YogaEarth. After commission, it was the exact amount of money I needed for March.

The Divine had delivered. *The Daily Love* had actually started making money.

Around that same time, Tommy discovered I was staying in a pool house and invited me to stay on his couch for a while. I took him up on it. His couch in Venice was way better than my eight-by-eight room in the Valley. But things kept getting better and better. Tommy's cousin lived in the guesthouse out back. He knew my situation and asked if I wanted to stay in his house rent-free for the month of August, when he'd be gone.

I took him up on it, and one year to the day after I had moved into the pool house, I moved into Tommy's guesthouse. To me, it was like moving into a mansion.

I had my own washer and dryer, bathroom, kitchen, and best of all, Wi-Fi! No more coffee shops. No more "borrowing" Internet from other people's houses as I walked the suburban streets.

I made a solid intention never to go back to that pool house.

During August of 2010, Tommy and his wife, Kia, taught me all about alkaline food, Kundalini yoga, and focusing on your breath. They showed me how important it was to get my body back in shape after what I had been through. Tommy became a new mentor to me. He introduced me to green juice—now *that's* an experience I'll never forget. We were at One Life Natural Foods in Venice, CA. He made me a big green juice, gave it to me with a smile, and said, "Down this." So I did.

And almost threw up.

Not the reaction Tommy was expecting! But he told me that as I started to alkalize my body, green juice would start to taste better and better. He was right; pretty soon all my body wanted was green juice and yoga.

All the while, the clock was ticking. I only had a month in the guesthouse. I knew I had to find another place to live. In perfect Divine order, another friend who I met through Agapi, Jan Shepherd, offered me her place.

Jan, Tommy, Agapi, and Sophie (who you will meet shortly) became my LA moms.

Jan is one wise woman. I would come to her with all my crazy ideas and visions, and she would say to me again and again, "Honey, you gotta stay grounded." I was great at vision but horrible at execution. Jan helped me bring my visions down to earth. She helped me to see that, in many areas of my life, I was just talking shit. I was doing too much "faking it" and not enough "making it."

I was also surrounding myself with people who didn't have my best interests at heart. One of them was a guy who wanted to run my business. He ended up moving to China after I had promised him a bunch of my company. I had no money to my name, and Jan gave me a few thousand dollars to pay him off and buy the company back. She has always been and always will be there for me—as I will be for her.

Jan was leaving for Europe just as Tommy's cousin was getting back into town, and she offered me her apartment in Beverly Hills. She would be gone a month, so I had another reprieve. At this point I had been "couch surfing" for a year and two months, all the while tweeting, e-mailing, and trying to get *The Daily Love* off the ground. *The Daily Love* had literally become my daily meditation—my spiritual practice.

The *TDL* audience kept growing each day, and each day I would work harder and harder. I was on a roll. I felt the hand of the Divine at every turn. I was being supported. It was like Joseph Campbell says: when you follow your bliss, "doors will open where there were no doors before, where you would not have thought there were going to be doors, and where there wouldn't be a door for anybody else." I could see my experiences as a version of the Hero's Journey, and I was getting more and more confident that, if I took a leap out into the unknown, following my bliss, the Divine would be there to catch me.

a man about town

The Daily Love was taking off. We now had all kinds of celebrities following us. Even while I was going through my shit, the social media audience kept growing.

One day, I connected with a man named Jason Binn (@JasonBinn), who is a media publishing king in New York City. He was the founder of Niche Media and *DuJour* magazine. He had found out about *The Daily Love* from Kim Kardashian, and his tweets mentioned people like Russell Simmons and Tony Robbins. There was something special about this guy, and I wanted to meet him. So I sent him a message on Twitter, and to my surprise he got back to me. We decided to get together the next time he was in LA.

A few months later we met for lunch at the Sunset Tower Hotel on Sunset Boulevard. I showed up with scruffy long hair and barely clean clothes; Jason showed up with fancy hair and a killer suit. But it didn't matter. I couldn't believe how loving and giving this man was. I told him that Kim Kardashian had loved *TDL*. He called Kim on the spot and told her we were having lunch, and she gave me some Love over the phone.

As the meal went on, Jason asked me, "Who inspires the *Daily Love* guy?" I told him that I had been watching a lot of Tony Robbins videos lately. Jason, in his very New York accent says, "Oh, Tony—hold on a sec." He picks up his phone and dials a number. A moment passes.

"Sage?" he says. (Sage is Tony's wife.) "Hey, it's Jason—is Tony there? It's important . . ." Another moment passes, and he says, "Oh, okay. Well, when he's back, have him call me right away."

Frankly I was grateful I wasn't about to talk to Tony Robbins! That was a terrifying thing to think about.

Lunch went on. Just as we were about to wrap up, Jason's phone rang. *Oh shit*, I thought to myself.

You guessed it—Tony.

"Hey, Tony," Jason says. "I'm here with Mastin. He runs @TheDailyLove on Twitter."

Tony said he knew about and followed me. Oh my God.

"Here, talk to him . . ." Jason says, handing me the phone.

"Hi," I managed.

"HEY, MASTIN, IT'S TONY, HOW ARE YOU? I'M THRILLED THAT MY WORK HAS INSPIRED YOU!" It was indeed that classic Tony voice. "HOW DID YOU FIND OUT ABOUT ME . . . ?"

A moment passed, and then I finally mustered something.

"Um, *Shallow Hal* . . ." It was true. For those of you who may not know, *Shallow Hal* is a movie, and Tony makes a cameo. (A super funny movie, BTdubs.)

Tony laughed, and I relaxed.

He invited me to his seminar "Unleash the Power Within," which was happening the following month in New Jersey. Jason said it would be perfect—I'd come to NYC, he and I would keep talking about how we could help each other, and we'd go to UPW together. I had no idea how I would pay to get to New York or stay there, but I said yes. It was on. I was coming to UPW as Tony's guest.

And just like that, I was being thrown in a whole new direction. I gave Jason a big hug and was on my way.

Around that time, Jan was coming back from her trip so I had to move out. A couple days before I needed to leave, I was with my friend Sophie at her house in the Hollywood Hills. Sophie is one of the sweetest women I know. I met her through Agapi, and we connected instantly. It was like we'd been friends for a lifetime. She asked me if I needed anything, and I told her I actually needed a place to stay. Out of nowhere she offered her extra bedroom.

I couldn't believe it—was this actually happening?

My situation kept getting better and better. First a pool house, then a guest house, then an apartment and now a house in the Hollywood Hills? It appeared my faith was growing too big for an eight-by-eight room. Each time I feared I was about to go backward, the Uni-verse would propel me forward into something even better.

I still remember the day I moved from Jan's apartment to Sophie's house. I was filled with guilt that I still had to rely on other people for help. Even though *The Daily Love* seemed successful, I was still broke—barely getting by. I felt like the longer this went on, the more of a burden I would become to the people who were helping me. I started to think I was a worthless person because I needed so much help.

I walked into Sophie's house that evening and was greeted by Sophie and her daughter Leah with a *huge* sign that they had made. It said:

WELCOME HOME

It took everything in me to hold back tears (I wasn't so good at showing my emotions back then). Since it was late, I gave them a huge hug and then went upstairs to my room . . . where I proceeded to bawl like a baby. I had made the drive from Jan's to Sophie's filled with guilt and shame. And right when I was starting to think I was a burden, they had made me feel so loved.

It was such a visceral experience of how we are loved by others more than we can possibly love ourselves. Giving is so important, but when we always give and never receive, we keep ourselves closed down. Giving is a powerful position to be in, whereas receiving is surrendered and vulnerable.

The timing was perfect for all of us. Sophie and Leah had decided that Leah was going to leave school and be unschooled. (I'm not exactly sure what unschooled is—it's not homeschooled, and it's not uneducated. It's more about letting the child do what lights them up.) Since Sophie was working, that meant Leah and I were spending a lot of time together. Once again the Uni-verse had sent me to someone who could help me, and someone I could help in return. We started to become a real family.

all your needs will be met

The Daily Love was making a small amount of money each month. Because I knew I could stay at Sophie's indefinitely, I felt free to spend the money I was making. Food no longer came from Trader Joe's—I graduated to Whole Foods, which was good, because I was all in on the alkaline lifestyle I had learned from Tommy.

My allergy to money was reversing itself. Just when advertising funds seemed to be drying up, I would somehow get a check from members of the *Daily Love* community. I must have received at least $5,000 in 2010 from Daily Lovers who sent me money as a thank-you. I never asked for it, but right when I needed it, as if on schedule, it would show up—generally in the exact amount I needed.

The journey of *The Daily Love* taught me how to truly surrender. In the process, the experience of life had started to change for me. When I first learned the concept of "surrendering the outcome" through the work of Caroline Myss, I was terrified. I was unsure of the future and scared about the past. But now I was living day to day. And day after day, I was being caught by the Uni-verse and supported.

I had exactly what I needed. I had gone a year and a half without a "real job," and the whole time I'd had a roof over my head, a mostly full stomach, and the money in my pocket that I needed. This way of living brought me more into the present moment than I'd ever been. Fear of the unknown started to transform into a sense of excitement and positive expectation. Whereas before I felt like I was being abandoned by God, I now felt like God and I were in this together. I had enough faith to let the uncertainty of my life yield positive results. I no longer lived in fear of the worst-case scenario.

In addition to *Star Trek* and *Star Wars*, growing up I was also a huge Indiana Jones fan. In the third film, *The Last Crusade*, Indy and his father go on a hunt for the Holy Grail. They are competing with the Nazis to find it. Indy's dad has been studying the Grail all his life and is an expert in the challenges that will come when one gets to the chamber where the Grail is hidden. There are three tests inside the chamber, the third being a leap of faith. The prophecy of the third test stuck in my mind for life: "Only in the leap from the lion's head will he prove his worth." My life had become one giant leap.

I remember the moment I decided to go all in on Plan A. It was back at the pool house, right after Kim K. tweeted about *The Daily Love*. I issued God a challenge.

If you gave me a gift, I said to God, *if you gave me a bliss to follow, if I'm supposed to help others and all this mess in my life is coming from surrendering to You, then I dare you to make me fail. If I fail it would be a total waste of talent. You and I both know you won't let me fail, so I dare you!*

That failure never happened, for two reasons. First, the support was always there. Second, I was always grateful for it when it showed up, no matter how small it might have seemed. I never said, *God, I asked for* abundance. *Why did you only send me $40 today?* I was grateful for what came, and saw it as a sign that I was moving toward my ultimate success.

The time came to head to New York to meet with Jason Binn and to attend Tony Robbins's Unleash the Power Within. Talk about a jaunt into the unknown! I had bought a ticket on faith to go to NYC, not knowing where the money was going to come from. Immediately after booking the ticket, I signed a client that paid for the ticket and more. A friend was letting me stay at her apartment in Jersey; so once again, the finances had fallen into place.

My only true hesitation about going to a Tony Robbins seminar was, of all things, the music. I am a music snob. You could say I like "cool" music. I had seen a lot of videos where Tony would play that 2 Unlimited song "Get Ready for This." I had hated that song since high school, and really didn't want to be forced to jump up and down while listening to such a cheesy-ass tune.

As I got closer to going, I noticed a bunch of resistance coming up. I started to think I shouldn't go. I was so scared that I told one of my friends that was also going that if that song was playing when we got there, I was leaving.

Jason wasn't able to make it to UPW after all, but I had a meeting with him at his office before going to see Tony. I was going to miss most of day one as a result, but I really wanted to catch up with Jason. When we met up, he took one look at me and sent me to his tailor on Madison Avenue and had a suit custom made for me. It was the first suit I'd owned in quite a while. I couldn't believe what a friend Jason was turning out to be. He and I spent the rest of the afternoon catching up, and then I rushed off to Jersey for UPW. I didn't want to miss the famous firewalk, which took place that first night.

Wouldn't you believe it? "Get Ready for This" was playing as we walked in. Not to mention that there were like four thousand people *freaking out* in the audience, while Tony was on stage dancing and getting the crowd excited. It felt like my personal version of hell. There was no way I was staying. I was *not* going to jump up and down to this song. And, I told myself, there was nothing wrong with me that I didn't want to, either!

My friend got me to stay. Tony had given us seats in the very front, after all. So I agreed to tough it out—for a little while. As soon as I got to the front and saw Tony doing his thing onstage, my irritation about the song fell away. In its place was an overwhelming sense of dread. I had been to countless concerts and had never felt this way. I wanted to throw up.

I watched for hours as Tony riffed onstage. I saw him doing interventions with people, taking them deep in a very short period of time. The audience was fixated on him. They wanted to be onstage, too. He was changing their lives. It was like the whole room fell into a trance.

As I looked around the room at the thousands of people who were there and at Tony just going and going, more and more fear came over me. I had to go outside for a moment and collect myself. I got still and calm. As I came back inside, walking from the very back to the very front, I felt a deep knowing start to rise up. It was that same knowing that had been there when I'd quit cocaine. It was the same knowing that was there every time I wrote.

"This is your destiny, Mastin."

I knew that the work Tony was doing up on that stage was the work *I* must do as well. It felt incredibly frightening to me at that moment. It all seemed so much larger than life. Impossible, even. I wasn't an onstage guy, I had long told myself. I was the guy *behind* the artists, the guy *behind* the computer. I was really happy hiding in the background.

But the more Tony spoke, the more transfixed I became—and the more *inspired* I was. The idea of working with people, live, was exciting and terrifying at the same time. It wouldn't happen immediately, but in that moment in New Jersey in 2010 the seed was planted. I literally had a front-row seat to the next stage of my own evolution.

As the night started to wrap up and we headed toward the firewalk, I realized I had missed something key: the training on how to walk on fire. I was led by some of the ushers to get in a certain line. Thousands of people were yelling "YES!" over and over again, all around me.

I saw that I was in Tony's line. He had just gotten off the stage and was lit up like a Christmas tree. He had so much energy—it was as if his whole body was red. Here was a human being living up to his full potential. I went up to Tony and introduced myself. I was surprised by how tall he was. When he gave me a huge bear hug I had to hug *up*—and I'm six-foot four!

I followed him out to the fire pit, where I was fourth in line. I had no idea what I was supposed to do. It was dark, there were loud drums, and the only light was the fiery glow of the coals in front of me.

Tony was yelling, "GET IN STATE! MAKE YOUR MOVE!"

I didn't know what that meant, but I saw the people in front of me yelling and moving their bodies—seeming to fill them with intensity before they made the walk. I caught on, and joined in. Soon, it was my turn.

Tony was to my right, and his already intensely red face was lit up by the fire in the darkness. He was yelling right in my ear, "Make your move! Make your move! Get in state!"

I tried.

He yelled again, "That's not it! Make your MOVE! GET IN STATE!"

I dug deep and found the most intense energy I could muster—the anger I still had toward John. I yelled and screamed. Apparently Tony was convinced because he yelled, "GO!"

And I walked across the fire.

Before I knew it, it was over.

I went to the last couple days of the seminar, spending half my time taking copious notes, and half my time watching how Tony communicated during his interventions. I wasn't sure what he was doing, exactly, but I knew I wanted to master it. On the third day of the seminar there was a point where Tony started to talk about the other events he offered. If I thought the 2 Unlimited song had triggered me, I had no idea what was coming next. I couldn't believe he was trying to "sell" people—right here, live and in person!

This was the part of the personal-growth world that I really hated. I had this idea that personal-growth people are just used-car salesmen underneath it all. In spite of everything I'd seen and learned that weekend, as soon as Tony went into his sales pitch, he became one of those used-car salesmen in my mind.

He went on and on about this thing called "Date with Destiny." It was another seminar, and it cost a lot of money—six or seven grand. Part of me really wanted to go, but I certainly wasn't rolling in cash like that. So take my preexisting prejudice for bs sales techniques in the personal-growth field coupled with resentment that I couldn't afford the next seminar—and you can imagine the cocktail that resulted. I projected all of my lack onto Tony and decided he was a very bad guy.

But as the seminar wrapped up, I couldn't stop thinking about Date with Destiny. Even the name itself sounded so cool! I really wanted to go, but I told myself to forget it—there was no way I could come up with the money.

The next day I had a meeting scheduled with Tony and Jason. It was awesome. Tony asked me about my life, and we ended up talking about Date with Destiny. Tony went into the same sales pitch that he'd made at the seminar—with the same intensity, even though it was just me in the room. I stopped him halfway through and said, "Tony, I don't have that kind of money; you are wasting your time."

Tony told me that he wasn't trying to sell me—*he wanted me to come as his guest.* My mind was blown. Tony's wife, Sage, was also in the room—and she and Tony spent the next five to ten minutes reinforcing how awesome Date with Destiny was.

He spoke to me with the same level of passion and intensity that he had in front of 4,000 people the day before, and did he want anything in exchange? Nope. He just wanted me to come. He was *that* passionate about it.

Of course I accepted . . . and quietly berated myself for judging Tony so harshly. Here I'd thought he was just bs-ing people onstage, but he actually meant all the things he said. This guy was the real deal. I felt so privileged that I had gotten a chance to be with him.

I had no idea how much my life was about to change.

— chapter 9 —

A DATE
WITH DESTINY

I believe life is constantly testing us for our level of commitment, and life's greatest rewards are reserved for those who demonstrate a never-ending commitment to act until they achieve. This level of resolve can move mountains, but it must be constant and consistent.

—TONY ROBBINS

I HAD A DATE WITH DESTINY, AND I COULDN'T WAIT. AFTER UPW I was already filled with inspiration to take my life to the next level.

Little did I know I was about to get bitch-slapped by Tony Robbins.

But I'm getting ahead of myself. I can tell you that DWD delivers on its promise; it was one of the most important weeks of my life. If I thought UPW was awesome, that week I got introduced to a whole other level of awesome.

It's impossible to break down everything that happens during the event, and I wouldn't want to ruin it for you. But I can tell you it's a game changer. So much so that I go back every year, and now I bring friends with me.

That said, I'd like to share a few key moments from that first Date with Destiny that changed me forever. The first was the realization that the majority of my action up until that point in my life had been motivated by the desire to be important—or "significant," as Tony would say. There's nothing wrong with wanting to be important. It's something we all need as human beings. But I saw that it was the *most important thing* driving my life. This realization was *huge* for me. It gave me the answer to a question I had been asking since my Hollywood dreams had faded: *God, why would you show me the heights of success and then take it all away?*

At Date with Destiny, I saw I had been taking a selfish journey. This reminded me of the very first self-help quote I ever saw from Stephen Covey: *"Seek first to understand, then to be understood."*

When I looked back over my life, I saw that every endeavor motivated by the need to be important or significant had eventually failed.

My career in the music business—I wanted to be the most powerful guy in the game.

The Love Yourself clothing company—I wanted to be "the" guy to bring self-love to the world, even though I didn't love myself.

And then it hit me: *The Daily Love* could go the same way if I wasn't careful. I realized how caught up I was in how many followers or "likes" I had—the more I had, the more significant I felt.

I also saw that my addictions in the past had stemmed from the stress of never feeling significant enough. That's one of the "benefits" of cocaine: I felt "significant" when I was on that drug. I thought back to my question, *God, how can I feel as good off the drugs as I do on them?* I saw for the first time that I had been doing drugs to feel good about myself—to feel important.

That was a huge *Aha!* for me. All the "failures" and "addictions" in my life were actually showing me how selfish my journey had been. And the stress and dis-ease had come from the selfishness.

I had gotten it backward. I was trying to go out and be important in the world at the expense of others. I wasn't actually focused on helping other people.

This even explained why my partnership with John had fallen apart: We were each driven to be the most significant player in the company. We hadn't been working together for the good of the organization as a whole. It was a power struggle that had brought down the self-love company! How tragically ironic.

Realizing all of this, I broke down during the seminar. I thought I had always been trying to do good in the world. How could I have gone 28 years without realizing I was just an insecure kid trying to be important, and going about it in all the wrong ways?

I've come to believe that when significance is our driving need, it can literally be lethal. Think about it: If you need to be number one all the time, how do you relate to other people? Isn't there always someone else more significant? How stressful is that?

I believe in healthy competition. When you are competing with someone in business, for example, it can make your company better because it encourages you to up your game and add more value for your consumers. But that kind of competition is totally different than basing your whole sense of self and identity on being number one.

When you live your life trying to be the best, it's a selfish journey. It is not heroic. According to Joseph Campbell, in *The Power of Myth*, the hero goes on the journey for the benefit of others: *"A hero is someone who has given his or her life to something bigger than oneself."*

Some hero I had been.

But I knew that I could change all that. I just had to switch it all around and make my driving need *contribution* rather than personal significance. If I could somehow figure out how to make serving other people and being Loving my driving need, my whole perspective—and my whole life— would change.

if you want to be happy, give and grow

The problem was that most of the success I'd seen had been achieved through fear and the drive for significance. I had never seen someone win who was contribution-driven.

Up until that point, I hadn't trusted life enough to let go of the need for significance. I wasn't sure whether I could trust life to support me if I changed my priorities. The underlying question that had been driving me my whole life was, *How can I be the most important person possible, so I can get the love I always wanted?* My new question had to become, *How can I serve others at the highest level possible?*

This was a hard switch to make. I had been in survival mode for so long it was difficult to focus on anyone but myself. But I realized that if I didn't take my focus from "me" to "serving others," my life would never genuinely change.

As Tony says: *"If you do what you've always done, you'll get what you've always gotten."*

So I had to change! But how? I decided to pray:

Dear God, please show me how to feel supported as I take the focus off of myself and place it on serving others. I don't know if I trust life enough to support me if I do, but I know with You all things are possible. Please show me the way.

The next breakthrough I had at DWD was when Tony had us go back to our earliest childhood memories. In mine, I was about four years old and my family lived in Fredericton, New Brunswick, in Canada. My mother needed major back surgery, so they sent her to Toronto. After a hellish stay in the hospital (I later heard she'd died on the operating table— thankfully she came back), Mom was flown back to Fredericton by medivac. I hadn't seen her in weeks.

I recall running down the tarmac to greet my mom. I had no idea she was in pain. I jumped on her in the stretcher and landed squarely on her wound. My mother just held me with Love, but everyone around us freaked out. Because of that response, I felt I had done something wrong.

At Date with Destiny I saw that at four years old I had made a key assumption that had been with me ever since, though I wasn't aware of it until now. I believed that when I expressed my Love, it hurt people. I had been operating based on this unconscious thought for most of my life.

This made so much sense to me. It explained why I wasn't able to really express myself, and why I thought getting up onstage was such a bad idea. If I got up there, some part of me believed I would actually hurt people in the process of trying to Love and help them. Imagine the formula I was working with: expressing yourself = causing pain to others.

The last thing I wanted to do was cause others pain. And yet I was dying to really express myself. I had been writing *The Daily Love* for years and had gotten so much feedback that my work was changing lives. But there was a part of me that didn't believe it, no matter how much positive feedback I got. The haters, on the other hand, I believed; they spoke my shame voice out loud. I was so deep in my shame that when others spoke that way to me, I needed no convincing. A part of me would actually chime in: *See, I told you so! You* are *worthless!*

I saw where this voice originated. It had come from a very innocent and real place—the moment I had jumped on my mother in an expression of Love, and it had caused her massive pain. From that point forward, I kept myself subdued so I wouldn't cause anyone else pain. As my Spirit called me into the unknown—called me to follow my bliss—this story was holding me back. It kept me in hiding from the world and my calling.

Combine the need to be the best all the time with a deep fear of self-expression and a simultaneous drive to grow, and what do you get? One very ego-driven, shame-based, unexpressed, anxiety-filled mess.

No wonder I was addicted to drugs and sugar and everything else! The pain of not expressing myself, while simultaneously needing to be number one, was literally killing me. I was beyond grateful that the Divine, God, the Uni-verse had enough Love for me to protect me during my lost years in Hollywood. I could have died so many different times, and yet by Grace I was still alive.

And I was equally grateful to be at this seminar—and to be able to make these realizations right now, in this lifetime.

man up

Things were starting to make sense. The third *Aha!* was that I had not yet learned how to embrace my masculinity. Because I equated expressing myself with hurting others, I had shut that down. Through a very powerful exercise at Date with Destiny, I learned how to reclaim my masculine side.

There is a difference between male/female and masculine/feminine. A *male* is a human with male genitalia. A *female* is a human with female genitalia. But masculine and feminine are energies—two sides of the same coin. Together they create the dance of the Uni-verse. You can think of masculine energy as "presence seeking freedom." That is to say, it is presence or stillness, a sense of firmness that is unwavering and always there. And the masculine *lives* (and dies) for freedom. Masculine energy has been dying for freedom since the beginning of time. Masculine energy also seeks freedom in the form of finishing a project, protecting and providing for those it loves, and sexual release. All these are the freedoms that masculine energy seeks. Feminine energy, on the other hand, is the opposite. It's "freedom seeking presence." That is to say, feminine energy has a sense of flow, a sense of openness, a sense of freedom that has no container or boundaries. It expresses for the sake of expressing. Feminine energy seeks the safety of masculine energy, because not until it feels safe can it fully express whatever it's feeling in the moment. So the goal of feminine energy is to feel safe, while the goal of masculine energy is to feel free. And we all have both masculine and feminine energy within us.

My problem was that taking care of my mother as I grew up taught me to be more feminine than masculine. I didn't know how to really be in my masculinity—to step into my purpose and hold space for the feminine. Up until this point, I was always the "best friend" of the girls I had met, but rarely their lover. I had been rejected so many times it hurt. I even wrote a blog on *The Huffington Post* about guys getting caught in the "friend zone"—the zone where you're always the friend and never the boyfriend. (Later *Wikipedia* picked up the blog and used it as a reference to define the "friend zone"—which was equally flattering and embarrassing. I'm linked to the friend zone for all eternity.)

You could say that up until DWD, I was a walking example of the friend zone.

But that week, Tony taught me about something he called *masculine presence*. He taught me about how to cherish a woman so deeply that she felt safe enough to open. He taught me how to be a man—a lost art, but one that is desperately needed in our world today. I stepped into—and actually accepted—my masculine, for the first time in a long time at Date with Destiny. And a new part of me came alive, a part I had never given myself permission to have before. My dating life would never be the same. In fact, I didn't know it then, but the love of my life was shortly on the way to me!

The final *Aha!* came from two classic bits of Tony wisdom. I still live by both of these to this day: *"Massive action is the cure-all"* and *"The quality of your life is the quality of your relationship to uncertainty."*

After I realized I needed to focus on service rather than significance, and after I realized I could actually help people when I express myself, Tony went on to drop these truth bombs.

I was taking *action* toward my dreams with *The Daily Love*. But I wasn't taking *massive action*. I was certainly not pushing far into the unknown. Up until that point I had been merely tiptoeing into the unknown, slowly but surely. I started to see it was because I didn't yet fully and completely trust life. I had faith, but I still equated the uncertainty of the future with death. And here, just as I was starting to trust life a little bit, Tony was asking me to up my game. Massively.

I knew he was right. I realized that I needed to become friends with uncertainty, and to take even more action. I needed to push consistently into uncertainty if things were going to change.

At the time, massive action looked like taking more risks. I needed to show myself, get out from behind the computer, start speaking, start doing more online programs, and start getting out into the world. I was *sooo* scared to do that, though. I liked the safety of being behind a computer. I liked being able to control things digitally and not have to see people face-to-face. There was a level of comfort I had gotten used to, but that comfort was thwarting my dreams. So I set the intention to do more things that would scare the heck out of me. I recalled first seeing Tony on stage at UPW and being so scared of stepping up in front of people, but I *knew* deep down that was what I had to do.

My whole paradigm shifted that week. I'd come to Date with Destiny as a significance-driven guy, afraid to really express himself, who was taking a "tiny bit" of action into the unknown. I left like a dog with my tail between my legs, licking his old wounds of significance and eagerly desiring to serve. It took a long time to actually embody these ideas (I'm still working on them to this day), but I had been cracked open and there was no going back. I had no more excuses—I could no longer say, "I don't know any better," and "No one ever told me."

In fact, I thought this was all I needed to hear; I was good to go. Well, as usual, I was wrong and still had more to learn. And this one was going to be painful.

cue painful ego death

The Tony Robbins bitch slap happened a week later.

I had a meeting set up with Tony at his home in California. I drove out there with all these ideas of how we could work together. I was so inspired by him. He was the first male role model I'd had since Luke Skywalker.

I arrived at his house and sat with him and Sage. We recapped my Date with Destiny experience. I told him about my significance revelation, about the revelation with my mom, and about the recognition that I needed to take action.

"Mastin," Tony said. "Do you know why it's taken you so long to become successful?"

"No," I replied. I really wanted to hear the answer.

"Because you're a love bug, and what you are doing is leading with Love. It takes a lot longer to build what you are doing when you lead with Love, but once you get there you will have a really solid foundation."

His words really comforted me. He went on to say that when I made the decision to not express myself at the age of four that it was actually a blessing. Really? How could that be?

Tony explained. "You got really good at taking care of a wounded mother growing up. Now, you are taking care of hundreds of thousands of wounded women. It was a perfect setup for your life's work."

This was mind-blowing to me. I had never thought about it that way.

Tony asked me what was next for me, and I started talking about Joseph Campbell's Hero's Journey. I told him I wanted to "die" to my fear and be reborn "fearless"—that I wanted to transcend my fear. (I probably sounded really pretentious when I said this.) Tony laughed, and then dropped some of the best wisdom I had ever heard.

"Mastin, for you to be happy you must always be growing," he said. "That means you will always be faced with uncertainty. It's totally natural for human beings to be afraid when things get uncertain. You won't ever be truly fearless, but you can learn to use fear as fuel to motivate you."

So much for my Campbellian death and rebirth.

He then proceeded with the bitch slap.

"Would you say that your model for the world is the Hero's Journey?" he asked me. I told him yes, absolutely.

"That totally ties into your significance," he said.

"How so?" I asked, starting to feel a little defensive and angry.

"Well," Tony said, "if you are the hero, what does that make everyone else?"

Ohhh, this really pissed me off. He had nailed me. Tony had pointed out that I was still a significance addict—that my very model for the world *proved* it.

He told me that this advice was the real reason I had come to see him—not all the ideas I had about us working together. We wrapped up the meeting and I left feeling so angry I could spit nails. For the next two weeks I was really pissed at Tony. But of course after I calmed down I saw that he was 100 percent right. I was only just starting to understand the "service" part of the Hero's Journey. I finally realized that yes, I was the hero, *but so was everyone else.*

I still use the model of the Hero's Journey for my work, but now with that crucial idea in mind. And I do my best to keep my focus on the contribution and service elements of the Hero's Journey—rather than the desire to be number one or the best.

I'm not saying it's easy. While I'd had an opening, I still needed to embody what I had learned. There are plenty of times when the drive toward significance creeps back into my life. But now when I see it, I nip it in the bud. I know I will be learning this lesson for the rest of my life.

this shit actually works . . . if you do the work

When you work with Tony Robbins—whether one-on-one or at one of his seminars—you can't *not* learn a bazillion lessons. When I think back to my first UPW and DWD experiences the question is really, what *didn't* I learn?

The first thing I learned is that personal-growth work is actually really important, and that not everyone is a slimy sales guy. I had been using my fear of being taken advantage of as a reason not to grow. Tony totally blew that fear out of the water.

I also learned that while I'd been totally afraid of taking Tony up on his offers to bring me to UPW and DWD, they'd turned out to be exactly what I needed. I am so grateful that I faced my fears and used them as "fuel."

After my encounter with Tony at his home, I created a new mantra: *"Unless you're in mortal danger, fear is a compass showing you where to go."*

When I'm speaking in my own seminars now, I often ask, "Who wants to live a fearless life?" Most of the room usually raises their hands. Then I say, "If you want to live a fearless life, stay in your comfort zone." Tony taught me that fear is not a bad thing; uncertainty is a natural part of life. We can spend so much time avoiding uncertainty and justifying our fear that we never actually change. I also learned that service and contribution is *everything*. One of my favorite Tony-isms is *"Power flows to those that serve."*

When I first came into contact with Tony and his teachings, I didn't trust life, myself, or God enough to believe this saying was true. I thought power was something to be acquired through stress and significance. Slowly I've opened to the truth that life really *does* rush to the aid of those who help other people. I've also learned that in order to help others, you must first take care of yourself.

When I changed my question from *What can I take?* to *What can I give?*, everything changed. This switch cleared a block to all the miracles that were waiting for me. Service, I've come to realize, is the currency of Spirit.

It was like Life was waiting for me to get that. Because once I did, everything changed for the better.

— chapter 10 —

A WIDE-OPEN BREAK

*Success is what happens when
you survive all your mistakes.*

— DAD

I HAD REACHED A POINT OF NO RETURN IN MY AWARENESS about life. I had to change.

The problem was, I had no idea how. I knew I needed to trust Life, but I was terrified to give up my own personal significance in exchange for serving others. It meant changing a lifelong belief pattern—that the more significant I became, the more I'd get the Love and success I desired. If I didn't focus on me, how would I get my needs met? Could it be true that I had to throw my old belief system away?

The hard answer was *yes*. This thought occurred to me: *In order to become anything, I have to risk being nothing.*

The honest truth is that I was so scared of failure that I never allowed myself to really try. I was so concerned with my own survival that I had turned selfish and borderline narcissistic. I had held myself back from really, *really* giving it my all because I was afraid that I was going to fail or die. My old ways no longer worked. I tried to go back, but all the power was gone. Forward was the only option—but how? I was still terrified of the unknowns in my future. But no one who's ever done anything awesome started out with the certainty of knowing what was going to happen. It's always been, and always will be, a simple leap of faith.

Well, when you don't make that leap yourself, life tends to force one on you, especially if you've been asking for it. I found this out the hard way, because as it turned out the Divine's answer to my prayer came in the form of a broken heart—and an exodus from my happy home with Sophie and Leah.

I'd been attending a 12-step group on love addiction, and had just ended a 30-day celibacy challenge. This meant no sex, no masturbation, and no flirtation for an entire month. Love addiction is a dis-ease where you make someone else your Higher Power. They seem so magical, so special, and so amazing that you give away all your power to this person and forget your own. It's so easy to do. The celibacy challenge is part of the process of recovery. It gives you a really clear view of how you spend your sexual energy. Your sexual energy is also your creative energy, so this was huge. I remember reading once in Napoleon Hill's book *Think and Grow Rich* that many men tend to become successful later in life because they spend the first part of their life wasting their creative energy on sexual pursuits. I had always been career driven, not wasting a lot of time and money there. But I was and still am a total Love Addict. It's so easy for me to give my power away to someone else, projecting Godlike qualities onto them. Since no one is perfect, the Love Addict always gets let down in the end—and crashes *hard*.

It's also amazing to see how much energy we waste flirting with other people. I know it sounds harmless enough, but when I stopped flirting for 30 days, I had an incredible amount of freed-up energy. I saw that I had been flirting as a subtle way to get other people's approval, and that it was an actual energy drain on them and me. My flirting wasn't as cute and innocent as it had seemed! It was amazing to see how I'd been spending my sexual energy in all the wrong places, and I was determined to do things differently from here on out.

Enter Jessica.

Jessica was an old friend who I'd had a little crush on a year or two earlier. She'd had a boyfriend at that time, but when I ran into her again at a Hollywood party, she was single. On paper she seemed like the perfect fit—artistic, creative, had a big heart, was all about teaching people self-love, and understood Hollywood.

Jessica lived a service-based life. She was always trying to help other people. She had a heart for the homeless and a Love for those who were having a hard time. We'd chatted all night at the Hollywood event and I'd left feeling inspired. I was especially intrigued to discover that Jessica had "given up boys for Lent"—she was basically on a "Love Cleanse" of her very own. To me, this felt like confirmation. We were definitely soul mates (hello, Love Addict).

That said, she was only on day 8 of 40. I had 32 days until I could ask her out!

But that didn't mean we couldn't be friends. So we spent a bunch of time together over the next few weeks.

Not like the Lent thing wasn't a dead giveaway, but at some point I discovered that Jessica was a Christian. The word alone was enough to send me into scary middle school flashbacks, but I liked her enough to remain open. She invited me to a Bible study in Venice, CA. I had zero interest, but for *her*—why not? I decided to go.

But that doesn't mean I wasn't scared. I was half expecting to be called "monkey boy" all night. Instead, what I found was a group of people so kind, so loving, and so cool they changed my view of Christianity in just a few hours. *These* were Christians? You have to remember, up until this point Christians equaled hypocritical jerks to me. But these people were different.

Lent came and went, and I still didn't have the courage to ask Jessica out. I was too afraid that she would say no (hello again, friend zone). But I started going to more and more Bible studies. I liked the people I was meeting there and what they stood for. It didn't hurt that Jessica was there, too.

My interest in Jessica even got me to go to church, which was a miracle. I had sworn off church a long time ago. What I discovered is that there are *cool* churches in LA. These were not the Kansas churches I knew. The congregants were hip, and the pastors were young and had style. They spoke my language.

Along with my new love of Christians came a new relationship with Christ himself. I felt a kinship with Jesus that

I hadn't known before. It was like I was falling in love with a guy I previously hated. As I started to see real friendship and Love embodied in the Christians around me, I started to make a distinction between human love (or lack thereof) and *God's love*. When the Christians of my childhood had made fun of me, I had blamed "God." I'd held God accountable for the actions of imperfect human beings. In other words, I had thrown the Divine baby out with the bathwater.

Now, going to Bible studies with Jessica, I saw that Jesus and I agreed on most points. His words and beliefs were totally aligned with everything I was writing about in *The Daily Love*. I had spent years and years dismissing the teachings of Jesus Christ because of what happened to me at Christian school. But now I was starting to see that there was actually a lot for me to learn here. I felt a sense of coming home the more I learned about Jesus, who He was, and what He stood for. It was totally different than what I had felt from Christians growing up.

What's more, every time I would hear someone talk about "Jesus" or use His name, I felt power. What I mean by that is I finally felt like I had found a path that worked for me. When I thought of Jesus, I felt at home. Jesus had become my Higher Power, a place of refuge and trust—my personal connection to the Divine. The more I learned about Jesus, the more I learned that He was the first true messenger of Grace in our world. That is to say, he delivered the message that we are always, and will always be, Loved by the Divine. Grace is a Divine favor. Jesus came to let us know that Grace cancels out karma.

Power was such a bad word for me for so long, yet now it had new meaning. As an ex-Hollywood manager, I equated power with greed, money, and ego. But the kind of power I felt in this reconnection to Christ was something different. It was big and eternal. It was the power of the heart, something that could move mountains. The old guilt and shame of my Christian upbringing was being washed away, and a new era of my awareness was being ushered in.

A book that really helped me understand Christ was *The Sermon on the Mount* by Emmet Fox. This book changed the game for me and Jesus. It's about the metaphysical teachings of Christ, and offers a different perspective than the typical Church dogma. Fox put Jesus into terms that I could understand.

He helped me see that the "Christ" is a level of consciousness. You can think about "Christ Consciousness" as the highest level of consciousness attainable by a human being (also called Buddha Consciousness, or simply "being Love"). Christ Consciousness doesn't mean that all is well all the time and you never suffer. If you look at the life of Christ, there was plenty of suffering, anger, and betrayal. As Joseph Campbell would say, Jesus was here to "participate joyfully in the sorrows of the world." Fox helped me see that many of us humans have missed the mark when it comes to understanding Jesus. We think that Jesus is "out there." But really He— and the Christ—are "within." Christ is something each of us can aim to embody in our own lives. Remember, all religion is a metaphor for the unexplainable. God is so big that no religion can claim ownership. Similarly, Jesus, Mohammed,

Buddha, and many other avatars that represent the nature of God are so big that no religion can claim them. They are all incredible teachers who point us back to the Love of the Divine. What we are seeking is not more knowledge of the Divine, but a Divine *experience.*

a brief disclaimer

Before I go on, I feel the need to insert a disclaimer. I am a Christian, but that's not the full story. In fact, I am a Christian *mystic.* What's the difference? I'm glad you asked. It means that my teacher is Jesus Christ, a man who came to Earth and embodied Love. But from the mystical perspective, Jesus is not the only teacher there is. The essence of Love can be expressed in many ways, through many different teachers. Whether it's being taught by Christ, Krishna, or Allah, Love is Love. Many humans have had the direct experience of Christ-level consciousness. That's what mysticism is about—seeking *experience beyond form.* That is to say, to the mystic, words matter less than feeling and experience. Remember the Zen teaching: Are you looking at the finger or the moon? Mystics look at the moon, no matter who is pointing.

So when I talk about Christ, please know that I'm talking about a level of consciousness. It doesn't matter who it's coming through. (When I'm talking about Jesus, on the other hand, I'm talking about a particular human being who embodied Christ consciousness in his life.)

It's easy to think that the only Christians in the world are those gun-toting NRA Republicans who are against equal marriage and think that if you aren't a Christian you are going to hell. You know, the ones who generally don't practice what Jesus preached.

That's not me.

I believe that when Jesus told his disciples to go spread the Gospel, he meant to embody Love—not beat someone over the head with a book you don't follow yourself. I think it's a tragedy that the life of Jesus has been taken over by a group of people who totally misunderstand His teachings. Jesus wasn't a "Christian." He was an awake human being. Too many people spend too much time looking at His finger, and not focusing on the moon.

So to recap, I honor all paths that lead to Love. My favorite path, the path I choose and the teacher that lights me up most, is Jesus. He was a rock star; a human being who managed to embody Christ-level consciousness even while remaining a human. I aspire to follow his example.

He was an incredible teacher who truly embodied Love, and His message has been distorted and perverted for centuries under the guise of religious dogma and oppression that serves only to bring power to institutions that fall short of embodying His teachings. There is a major difference between the institutions that claim to represent Christ and the man himself. Jesus was simply a human being who awoke to the truth of Love. And that's why *I* Love *him*. I don't claim to be a part of any church or subgroup, I simply Love Jesus. It begins and ends there. Jesus needs a new publicist, in my mind. He really was an incredible dude who set an example any of us can follow.

find God, lose the girl. fair trade?

So I had three JC's in my life by now: Jesus Christ, Joseph Campbell, and Jessica Chaplin.

And one of them was about to leave.

I had started praying to Jesus, and my new prayer had been, "More of You and less of me." My anthem was the song "Mighty to Save" by the Christian band Hillsong. The line that moved me most was, "Savior . . . He can move the mountains . . . my God is mighty to save. He is mighty to save . . . I surrender."

Powerful words.

I wasn't sure why, but I had started to sense that I had a mountain ahead of me. I could feel change on the horizon, and I was terrified of what was to come. I kept up with my daily prayer, "Thy will be done. More of You and less of me." But when I first heard Hillsong's "Mighty to Save" at church, I felt like it was meant just for me. I bawled.

I listened to it over and over and over again in the car. Each time I heard it, my fear was lessened just a little bit and I found just a little more faith.

This song got me through the next wave of uncertainty in my life.

I had been at Sophie's for nine months. It had worked out great, but I sensed that I needed to move on. After almost two years of couch surfing, I was ready to step up and pay my own way.

Right before I was going to move out, Jessica and I went to dinner. Finally, after months of waiting for the right moment to tell her how I felt, I professed my love to her. To my dismay, she told me she was still not over her ex.

It was like she shot an arrow directly through my heart. How could this be? We had so much in common. She had brought me back to Christ! She and I made total sense on paper. It was hard for me to digest that my feelings were not reciprocated.

I told Jessica that the idea of not being able to date her was painful enough that I wanted to take some space. She had become my Kryptonite. Remember my Love Addiction tendencies? Well, she had become my Higher Power without her even knowing it. I couldn't make a move in my life without trying to fit her into the plan. I had lost myself. I needed to find my way back to "me" again.

When I dropped her off that night, I saw her ex parked outside her house. It was just his silhouette, but it was enough to break my heart. And this time, it was a wide-open break.

Jessica had helped me find a faith that was perfect for me. She and I were so well matched. How could she not see how great we could be together? I was shattered. Luckily for me, Sophie and Leah were out of town that weekend. For the next three days I had a shouting match/meltdown with God.

"Why!?!?!" I screamed, crying. How could I have created *The Daily Love*—something that inspired so many people, most of them women—and yet still be denied the Love I so wanted? I was crying for Jessica, but I was also crying for every girl who had ever said "Let's just be friends." By that point there had been almost a hundred of them in my life.

I'm grateful I was home alone, because I cried gallons of tears over those three days.

I was feeling anger toward my new role model, Jesus. What's more, after the three days, I realized that I was confused. Did I really Love Jesus—or had it just been a show for Jessica? The euphoria of being around her was confusing. Was I feeling Love for her—or for Him?

I could see a pattern that had appeared many times before: me, twisting and molding myself to get the approval of a woman. I had become a different person around Jessica. A yes-man. And it wasn't the first time I'd done that. It had happened time and time and time again. That weekend I decided to change. Going forward, I would show women the total truth of who I was—even if I thought it was ugly.

I got two gifts from this heartbreak: I got myself back, and I got Jesus. These two things had been missing from my life up until that point. It was a slow path, but I decided I had to be myself. No more bending to please other people, no more making someone else my Higher Power.

Just like the girl who'd handed me the Caroline Myss CD, Jessica had given me the gift of faith. I didn't know where it would take me, but I knew the ride wasn't over.

I remember having another "conversation" with the presence I had become so familiar with about why Jessica denied me. The answer I got back was that something better was on the way. I couldn't see how that was possible, because Jessica seemed so perfect. But I was willing to find out.

leaving the nest

It was time for me to leave the comfortable nest of Sophie's house and venture into the great unknown. I had no idea what was going to happen next. Where would I live? How would I find—and pay for—that home? As usual, the Universe delivered.

I had made a new friend named Ryland a few months earlier after watching his film *May I Be Frank*. Ryland was a co-owner of the famous vegan restaurant Café Gratitude. He had just moved from San Francisco to LA to open the first Café Gratitude in Hollywood. I felt like he was a kindred spirit, so I reached out and we became fast friends. I told him it was my dream to live in a big house with a lot of people who were all on a spiritual path. Well, the realization of that dream was on the way. Right when I needed to move out of Sophie's house, the opportunity came.

Ryland and many of the servers at Café G all lived together in two houses in Downtown LA. Ryland invited me to come live with him as part of the Café Gratitude family. I started out in a small room, paying a very reasonable price for LA, but I was terrified. I still wasn't sure *The Daily Love* would cover my expenses. I spent the first month so stressed-out about paying rent that I drove myself crazy and started eating to relieve my anxiety. Financial uncertainty is my biggest trigger. I can handle public speaking, haters, rejection—but I have a special kind of freak-out when faced with financial uncertainty.

Thankfully, one day it hit me that the overwhelming amount of stress I was feeling amounted to a $700 fear. *Seven hundred dollars was running my life.*

Don't you think the Uni-verse can handle $700? I asked myself. I realized my focus had been all wrong. I was putting all my attention into my fear of not having, rather than putting it on service to others. So I turned my attention to contribution, and asked a new question.

How can I improve the lives of others, right now?

I decided I could take on more one-on-one mentoring clients. So I set my intention to find three $200-a-month clients who would help me cover my rent.

By the end of that first month, I had made $2000 mentoring clients. I couldn't believe it. Life was supporting me in miraculous ways.

Better yet, my clients were having breakthroughs. They were coming back over and over, and referring me to their friends. Suddenly, I was paying my own way through life based on making contributions—all because I'd turned my focus away from my "money problem" and toward serving others.

I started to see that I didn't need a "job"—what I needed was income. And income was coming in. I had never really made money in a way that served other people, especially not while doing something I loved so much.

I remember Fourth of July that year; Ryland invited me up to Ojai for a party. As we entered the house through his friend's fully stocked kitchen, he bellowed out what would become my new mantra: "We are abundantly supplied!"

It was like a message from God: *Mastin, you are abundantly supplied—you don't need to worry.* It felt like God had my back.

But that clarity was momentary. I was still operating from a mind-set of insecurity. I believed that life wouldn't support me if I served, even though all around me there was evidence to the contrary. Around this time I was also trying to get investment funding for *The Daily Love*, but nothing was coming through. It seemed like no matter where I went, investors weren't interested. I remember getting feedback from one investor in LA who said, "Your investment deck is too feminine." An investment deck is a PDF file you show to potential investors in your company. I guess he was so used to seeing boring numbers and charts that a little style threw him off. (Little did he know that *The Daily Love*'s audience is 93 percent women.)

One such unsuccessful meeting took place on the Santa Monica promenade—a boardwalk filled with shops, street artists, musicians, panhandlers, and a variety of other businesses. As I walked out of the office and down a few steps to the street, I heard a familiar tune—a guitar riff that had been burned into my mind over the last few months.

I looked up. Directly ahead of me was a young Asian man with a guitar, and he was playing "Mighty to Save."

I felt chills up and down my spine. Then I broke down. Yep, I started bawling right there in the middle of the promenade.

How could this be happening? I asked myself. Why was this musician right in front of me, and why wasn't he playing Miley Cyrus or Lady Gaga like the other street musicians? I felt like I was being firmly held by the Divine. I took it as a powerful sign to keep going.

A few weeks later an invitation came that would again change my situation. Some of the Café Gratitude people were hosting an event called Grateful Fridays. It was an attempt to combine spirituality and the Hollywood club scene, and it was being produced by people that I lived with. For the first event they had asked our friend, singer Jason Mraz, to play a set. And they asked me to open for Jason with a talk.

I was terrified. Me . . . speak? I'm a blogger, not a speaker.

But then I remembered my Tony Robbins experience. I knew it was time for me to come out from behind the laptop. So I accepted, even though I was terrified.

I practiced my speech for days. I decided to focus my talk on Joseph Campbell—and how to face your fears like a hero. (Cuz, you know, that's exactly what *I* was doing to get up and give this talk.) The day of the event, I ran into Jason before the show and revealed how scared I was. He told me I was great, and that I would do a great job. He was so gracious. Here's a guy who has played in front of crowds of 18,000, and I was stressed about 50 people!

As I headed out to the event, I started to have the same feeling I'd had before the *What the Bleep?!* conference—like something was about to change for me.

This time I wasn't dreaming about meeting a girl; I thought

it would have to do with my spiritual journey. Maybe I was going to be given a new self-help book?

I had very detailed notes, but to my own surprise I threw them out as I got up to speak. Something else wanted to come through. For the next 30 minutes I just talked, and had no idea what the hell was coming out of my mouth. I hoped these people thought this weird, inarticulate blogger kid was making some kind of sense.

Apparently they did, because at the end they all clapped. And it didn't even seem like one of those polite claps, it felt like genuine applause.

After my talk, we did a closing circle. I put my arms around the people next to me and my left hand touched the shoulder of a girl sitting one person over. It sent shivers through my body when I made contact.

After the closing circle, a beautiful, brown-haired, green-eyed girl approached me. Her energy was so open, so feminine, so sexy, and so present. The second she came up to me I heard a voice say, *Don't you dare break her heart.* I didn't even know who this person was, or what that voice meant, but I was paying attention.

Her name was Jenna, and she'd been reading *The Daily Love* for a while. She had moved to LA about a year ago and had come to see me give my very first talk with one of her friends.

We were together for the rest of the night. From the moment I met her, I never wanted to be away from her again. It was impossible for me to leave her. I used my special skills of persuasion to convince her friend to let me drive her home.

It was a 30-minute drive to her house. We left at 11 P.M.,

and she didn't walk through her door until almost 4 the next morning. We sat in the car and talked for over four hours. It was amazing and very odd.

Why odd? As I said, after Jessica I had decided never to censor myself again. And that night, I didn't. It was entirely new for me. I must have asked Jenna a thousand different questions about her life—what she believed, what she wanted, etc. I held nothing back. I kept waiting for her to reject me and give me a self-help book, but that never happened. Finally, it seemed the inner voice that told me my life was going to change before an event was actually talking about a girl!

By the end of the night, I thought she was amazing. She, on the other hand, thought I was crazy. But I was determined not to leave without a kiss. I didn't want to be in the friend zone this time. I knew it would be hard because I had probably scared her away with my million questions, but I was going for it.

"I really want to kiss you," I told her.

"That's not going to happen tonight," she said.

"Do you feel that if I kiss you it means I don't respect you?" I asked. (It was the first and only time in my life I've used my knowledge of how women think in order to seduce one. And BTW, Jenna knew what I was up to.)

"Yes, I would," she said.

"I could never view kissing you as a diminishment," I assured her—and then swiftly went in for the kiss. Surprisingly, she kissed me back.

The risk had worked. It was on.

I walked Jenna to the door and then drove home the happiest man in the whole world. As I got home, I thought to myself: *When you meet the Love of your life, it will make sense why it didn't work out with anyone else.*

Around that time I realized that *The Daily Love* was going to be late that day. I generally write it the day before, and it goes out at 4 A.M. Pacific Time. That day it went out at 4:30 A.M. instead—and for good reason.

I was, of course, very excited to see Jenna again. On one of our early dates I wanted to make sure she knew I liked her—and I wanted to make sure she hadn't changed her mind about liking me, too. I took her to the Griffith Observatory and we looked out over the city of Los Angeles at sunset. I can remember holding her as the sun went down over the Pacific and feeling a peace that surpassed all understanding; I was home.

In that moment I knew that Jenna was the reason it hadn't worked out with anyone else up until this point.

The reason why I was so drawn to Jenna wasn't just because she is ridiculously beautiful. We also got each other. I had never felt so *seen* by anyone in my whole life. She was smart, intuitive, and led with an open heart. I had never met someone who it was so easy to be with. I didn't just want her, I was in sync with her, and she with me. From the moment we first met, it felt like a new unit had been created. We were a perfect match on all levels.

When we surrender to Divine will, things may not make sense. And when you're talking about Divine will in relationships, it gets even more confusing. Because it's not just about your timing, it's also about the timing of the other person.

It hadn't made sense to me why it was taking so long to find the perfect partner. But I didn't factor in that the perfect partner—in my case, Jenna—was on her own journey to get to *me*. It wasn't happening on my timetable, but when she arrived there was no doubt I'd found her. (It helped that I had done work with Arielle Ford about a year earlier to make my soul mate wish list, and Jenna is everything on the list.) It was as if God had graciously handed me the most amazing woman in the whole world. As it turned out, it happened at just the right time, too. If it had been even a week earlier, we might not have seen each other. I was still healing from the ending with Jessica.

I now see that through the heartbreak over Jessica, my heart was being *opened* for Jenna.

Sometimes the heart must break in order for it to open.

I wrote a poem about heartbreak and it perfectly fits my experience with Jenna:

> *The heart breaks*
> *And the Soul takes flight*
> *Into the dark night*
> *To illuminate its Light*
> *And welcome dawn*
> *And a new day's delight.*

Jenna was worth waiting for. She was worth all the risks I took with *The Daily Love,* and she would have been worth enduring a thousand more heartbreaks if that's what it took. She was my new day's delight.

And with that, the contribution train was about to leave the station.

— chapter 11 —

A SECOND
SECOND CHANCE

The Universe specializes in redemption.

—ANON

The Daily Love WOULD NOT BE WHAT IT IS TODAY WITHOUT Jenna.

I write *The Daily Love*, but Jenna *is The Daily Love*. She is my grounding force, the demonstration of Love in my life. She is a gift that I have the privilege of waking up to each and every day. Jenna has Loved me in spite of myself. She has been patient, kind, empathetic, and totally there for me on every level. She inspires me to be a better person and has shown me how to live with an open heart. Before I met Jenna, Love was a concept that I could comprehend, but certainly wasn't embodying. Each day, Jenna has showed me what Love is, what it looks like, and how it acts. Jenna is my teacher, my best friend, my Lover, and my partner in crime. When I am with Jenna, I feel like I've come home. She was worth waiting for, worth hurting for, worth being broken up for, and worth all the pain and personal growth I went through.

If there is anything I regret in my life, it's a moment that came about a month into our relationship when I did something really stupid.

By that point I was elated to have finally found a person I could Love as much as Jenna. But I was also terrified. My heart was open but my defenses were up. (*Way* up.) Things were great, and yet I was having a hard time allowing them to be great. Jenna was the answer to my prayers. She Loved me deeply and completely. But I had never felt a Love like that, and it challenged my closed heart. It challenged all the walls I had put up. Turns out, after all the heartbreaks, setbacks, and disappointments, I was scared to open up again. I talked about it all day long, but I hadn't yet done it. In the past, my "relationships" had been temporary at best—fleeting desires of the flesh that were fun in the moment, but meant nothing. As soon as they got "real," I bailed to maintain control.

I like being in control. But around Jenna, I couldn't be that way. I had to grow. I had to admit my fears and my wrongs. I had to open up. I came to see that, after so many years of hurt and a ton of scar tissue, opening your heart can sometimes feel like death. And in a way it *is* death—death to the ego, death to the fear that keeps it closed, death to the possibility of escaping. As I would come to find out, all of these things are worth killing off for Love. But there at the beginning, I was scared. The deeper Jenna and I got, the more I wanted to run. And for a split second, I did.

I broke up with her.

A few days afterward, I got a text from Jenna. It was awesome, because I had been resisting my heart's desire to reach out. My fearful ego was too prideful. When the text came in and I saw her name, my heart lit up. But the text didn't say what I thought it would say. It said something like, AT WHOLE FOODS, DO WE HAVE TIME TO EAT BEFORE THE MOVIE? She and I didn't have plans. Wait a minute. Who the hell was she texting with? Another guy? So quickly? Had she meant to text him but then texted me? I couldn't handle it, so I texted back HI :-). She texted me back and I kept texting her, trying to find out what was going on. Turns out she was going on a "friend date" with her friend Michael. We were the only M's in her phone and she had "accidentally" texted me. (I believe it was a cosmic "accident"—the Uni-verse getting us back together!)

The next day I got over myself (it's hard 'cause I'm so tall, you see) and called her. At the time I did, we were both in grocery stores and buying similar things. I was there for Haas avocados, peppermint oil, eggs, coconut oil, and kale. We'd also seen the same movie that day (*The Help*). While watching the movie, I'd kept wishing Jenna was there next to me. I even remember that inner voice saying to me, *You asked for a girlfriend just like her and instead you are alone. She is out there and you can still grab her.*

So I grabbed her and didn't let go.

Well, almost. There was one other time, a little bit later, when we got into an early-couple fight. I don't remember what it was about, but I remember that we were arguing outside her house in my old and raggedy Jeep Grand Cherokee.

Finally I had decided it would be better to spend the evening separately, and perhaps break up. But my Jeep had other plans. It decided to die as I tried to drive away. I had no money to catch a cab home, so the only choice was to stay with her.

Months after the Jeep fight, I got an intriguing e-mail from my friend Marianne Williamson. She told me that Jenna and I had been in her morning meditation and asked if we wanted to come in to see her. Marianne offers counseling on all kinds of spiritual matters. Of course, we said yes.

When we got to her house, she ushered us into her living room. This was sacred territory. We sat down and Marianne asked us directly how our relationship was doing. As Jenna started to describe her experience, I found myself shrinking. I couldn't believe what she was saying. Apparently I was acting in a way that was pushing Jenna away! Hearing that, especially in front of someone like Marianne who I respect so much, made me embarrassed and sad.

But I couldn't deny that what Jenna was sharing was the truth. I clearly had a ways to go in terms of really understanding what Love was. Marianne then turned to me and with a ton of patience and compassion said, "Now, honey, you know I love you . . . right?"

Generally speaking, whenever someone says something like this, it's swiftly followed by a deep punch to the ego.

"Mastin," Marianne said, "you're acting like an asshole."

Boom—there it was. And she wasn't finished.

"You aren't a bad person, but there's a bunch of little cuts that are going to tear this relationship apart. Look at

Jenna—she is shiny and very beautiful. If you don't see how shiny she is, someone else will."

I had nothing to say except, "I'm sorry and you're right."

It was the second biggest wake-up call of my life.

Marianne Williamson hadn't called me an asshole, exactly. She said I was *acting* like one. But it was tough love, and I needed it.

How funny—the guy who was helping people find Love wasn't following his own advice! I had to start doing better. I had to take a risk and let Jenna's Love in. That was it; I set my intention there. I had worked so hard to find Love; now I had to become the person it took to keep the Love I had found. I had to admit when I was scared rather than lashing out emotionally. I had to trade passive-aggressive behavior for an open heart.

It's painful and scary to grow up, but that's what I had to do. Otherwise I'd risk losing her forever.

Part of that, for me, meant taking my faith to the next level.

I'm so grateful for accidental texts, Jeeps that break down, and friends with a great meditation practice. The Uni-verse wouldn't let me let go of her. My friend Tommy insists that Jenna should be canonized for being with me—and I agree. I am blessed to be with the most patient woman in the world.

Jesus and Jenna

It was time to get serious about my spiritual path. I had been baptized as a child, but I hadn't done it for myself; I'd done it for my parents and the Church. I hadn't really meant the words I'd said. So I decided to literally take the plunge—publicly announcing my faith through baptism.

I used to think that baptism was meaningless. It was only water; what good would it do? But, after reading a lot of Joseph Campbell, I saw that there is great power in ritual, especially when the person undergoing the ritual believes in the power of it. So, I saw this baptism as an opportunity to be reborn. I wanted to let go of fear. I wanted to step into being a real man. I wanted to live with an open heart and trust God, come what may. I was ready to commit my life to serving others instead of being selfish. All this was my intention for baptism—a fresh start and a shower for my soul. If I was going to do this, I was going to be all in and *believe* that it was a rebirth. That belief was the key.

My friends at church were happy I was getting baptized, and Jenna was there to see it, too.

From the moment my head went underwater in the baptismal pool at Basileia Church in Hollywood, I felt renewed. It was symbolic, yes, but a very powerful symbol. I was allowing myself to be new again. When I came up out of the water and saw Jenna it was like it all became clear: she was God's Love in my life. But for me to be God's Love in *her* life, I had to get my priorities straight.

I realized it was time to put Jesus at the head of all my affairs: *The Daily Love*, my relationship, my finances, and everything else. To me, this meant that I would focus on serving others, doing my best to embody the Love that Jesus showed us (even though I fail all the time), and continuing to surrender the outcome to my Higher Power.

The request I made in my relationship with Jenna was, "Show me how to Love her like you do." I'm still learning how to live up to that prayer today, but I can tell you we are getting better and better. The seed that was planted that day has taken time to unfold. Perhaps the greatest post-baptism lesson I've learned is that the best way to truly Love someone is to really listen and be present. There are so many opportunities for me to get distracted! When I catch myself, I do my best to come back to the present moment and just *be* there for her.

After I got baptized, I started to become more myself and took a step closer to being in my heart. I like to think that what's happened in my life since that moment would not have been possible without Jenna and Jesus.

One day I was in Jenna's apartment in Hollywood and I got an e-mail from someone at "Harpo.com." It seemed like spam. There's no way the real Harpo Studios (Oprah's company) would be e-mailing me, right?

But as it turned out, it was real. Morgan, a producer, had reached out because they were thinking about getting me involved with a new show they were creating called *Oprah's Lifeclass*. I wasn't sure exactly how they had found me, but *Lifeclass* sounded awesome—Oprah wanted to create the world's largest personal-growth classroom. It was a huge honor to be considered. I mean, I was just a little blogger from LA who wrote in Coffee Bean and Starbucks! Morgan and I got on the phone and totally gelled. We talked for over an hour. I felt like I had found a new friend. Soon she introduced me to someone else who became a dear friend—a woman named Maya.

Maya works at Harpo in digital marketing. We got on the phone and I was shocked to find out that she was a *Daily Love* fan. Could it be that *The Daily Love* had found its way into the hallowed halls of Oprah's company? That seemed too good to be true, but apparently it was. Maya and I became fast friends.

Soon the date was set. I was going to be an official Skyper on the first season of *Oprah's Lifeclass*. Being a Skyper meant that as the show was going on, I would be live on camera via Skype. I'd get to ask a question to Oprah and her guest—Eckhart Tolle.

Oprah's team sent me a fancy Skype kit, including a high-falutin microphone, a swanky camera, and my very own Oprah laptop with all the necessary software pre-installed. It took us three days of testing to get it all set up, and I had to borrow office space with a stronger Internet connection. If I'm honest, all the prep was making me nervous. I couldn't believe that I was going to talk to Oprah Winfrey and Eckhart Tolle live on TV!

The show started with a bunch of prep by the show's producers. Oprah welcomed everyone to *Lifeclass* and introduced Eckhart. My heart started to beat like a jackhammer. This was *really* happening—to *me*. Oprah and Eckhart started talking about all kinds of spiritual matters. But I wasn't paying attention; I was too nervous to take any of it in. I was just waiting for "the" moment. My palms were getting sweatier and sweatier. Finally, after what seemed like forever, Oprah cut to me. It was beyond surreal to hear Oprah say my name and the words *The Daily Love*. In that moment, *The Daily Love* became concrete to me. Up until that time, it had still seemed like the far-off dream of a boy running around a lake in Los Feliz, mad at his former business partner. But in that moment it felt like that dream had come into full expression.

I was flushed with excitement as I started to ask my question. I was on top of the world . . . until Oprah started talking to Eckhart in the middle of my question. I saw that they had cut away from me. Wait—what happened??

Sound issues, as it turned out. I'd been mouthing words on camera for about three seconds before they cut away. How embarrassing! First I'm on top of the world, then, just moments later, in hell. What could I do but let it go? So much for my big debut on *Oprah's Lifeclass*! Luckily, as I was driving home that night, I got a call from Morgan. She said they wanted to have me on the following night with Iyanla Vanzant.

Redemption!

The second night went smoothly, and as a result of the snafu Oprah said the words *The Daily Love* on camera *two days in a row*. It was almost more than my nervous system could handle. I left that night filled with a buzz—a buzz I had previously only felt when I was on drugs.

Wait—it was happening! My life was starting to feel as good *off* the drugs as it had *on* the drugs!

Since then, I've developed a practice. When I am having peak moments of Love and gratitude, I now say a silent prayer to God: "Thank you for this feeling. I'm so grateful. If it's Your will, I'd like more of this feeling, please." I have no idea what circumstances it will take to keep that feeling coming, so I no longer pray for circumstances. Instead I pray for the feeling itself.

I didn't think it could get any better than being on *Life-class* with Eckhart (even with the fail) and Iyanla, but destiny of an even greater magnitude was on the way.

a chance to walk my talk

Before I continue, I need to tell you a story.

One day, back while I was couch surfing at Tommy's house, he'd told me there was a man I needed to meet. This guy, Tommy said, had a big social media presence like I did. At the time, I had about 200,000 followers on Twitter. Remember, this was before Tony Robbins had come into my life, and before I'd learned about the concept of "significance." Back then, my Twitter following *was* my sense of self-worth. I was proud of it and I didn't like it when anyone else had a following as big as—or God forbid, bigger than—my own. I had done a lot of research, and at the time I believed I had a bigger following than anyone else in the self-help space except Deepak Chopra.

So when Tommy told me that this guy, Eric Handler, had a Facebook account with 600,000 likes—I was not happy for him. My self-worth crashed hard, because I wasn't number one anymore. *Who was this Eric guy, and what made him so special?* I wondered.

Tommy wanted to set up a meeting, but I declined. My pride couldn't take it. It was months later when I finally got over myself. He was a great guy, of course. But even so, I was defensive and quiet. I didn't like the idea that his site,

Positively Positive, had drawn more followers than *The Daily Love*. I felt threatened and intimidated.

Cut to a few months after *Lifeclass*, when I get a call from Maya at Harpo.

"Great news!" she said. "We want to invite you on *tour* with *Lifeclass* to blog at our live events!"

I was stunned. Was this really happening? Of course, I said yes.

Then she asked me a question that would put me up against all of my demons.

"Do you know any other self-help blogs with good followings that we should invite along?"

Tell her about Eric and Positively Positive! said my heart.

"No—but let me think about it," said my mouth.

I felt like crap. Was I really going to not tell them about *Positively Positive*?

All my fears came up. *They would find out about* Positively Positive *and then fall in love with Eric and fall out of love with me.* Lack and insecurity ruled. I knew what I had to do, but I couldn't bring myself to do it. So I did what any ego-driven person trying to live with an open heart would do: I called in reinforcements. I picked up the phone and dialed Tommy, who I knew would steer me in the right direction.

Thanks to him, I called Maya back and told her about *Positively Positive*. She was so excited she asked me to reach out to Eric myself and extend the invitation.

So I called Eric and told him the truth.

"Buddy, I have a confession," I said. "I'm intimidated by you. But I'm going to stop all that right now, because Oprah's people want you to come on tour with *Lifeclass*."

Naturally, Eric was stoked. Surprisingly, so was I.

I ended up inviting both Eric and my friend Mandy Hale from @TheSingleWoman on Twitter to blog on the *Lifeclass* tour. None of my fears came true; in fact, inviting Eric was a game changer for my life. The day before the final night of *Lifeclass*, Eric and I were in the hotel lobby in Toronto. Eric had started a conversation with two women and I had joined them. We were having a great time, telling stories and joking around.

The women asked us what we were doing the night after the final show. Neither of us had plans. It turns out that these women ran Oprah's office, and they invited us to the after-party. The *Lifeclass* bloggers weren't originally supposed to go to the party, but now were invited, too.

That's where I first met Oprah. And meeting Oprah that night ultimately led to me being invited to be on her TV show *Super Soul Sunday* several months later.

And none of that would have been possible without Eric Handler.

It's amazing how life works. My fear that Eric was going to steal my thunder turned out to be untrue. And meeting Oprah actually resulted in great things happening—some of which were beyond my wildest imagination.

a true role model

If I could be like anyone in the world, it would be Oprah. As you will see, she is extremely grounded, open-hearted, warm, present, and living in service. Really, she's everything I've ever wanted her to be and more. I've met many different celebs and successful people in my life, but none compare to her.

One morning I was at the gym, and as usual I didn't have my phone with me. (The gym is the only time I don't check my Twitter and e-mail.) When I got back to my phone, I saw that my Twitter stream had blown up during my workout. It seemed that Oprah had publicly invited me to have lunch with her at her home in LA—that very day! I had no idea why. Of course I said yes.

I grabbed Jenna and we changed clothes at the gym. We thought about what to bring Oprah as a gift—what could we possibly bring that she didn't already have? We decided on flowers. As we sped up to her house we were filled with excitement, disbelief, and a little fear. But soon we were knocking on her door. She answered it herself and greeted us with a big smile.

We ate a delicious lunch, drank freshly made almond milk, and had a great conversation. We talked about how important it is to feel like you belong and many other things. Then we went for a walk around her property.

I was about to get another major life lesson.

As we were walking through the woods, Oprah grabbed my arm. She pointed to a tree in the distance and said, "You see that guy? He almost didn't make it." I was having a hard time finding the injured tree, but soon I zeroed in on it. It was small and unremarkable—nothing I would otherwise have noticed.

"We've been helping that tree out for a while now, and I think it's gonna make it," she said.

I was flabbergasted.

Who cares about one little tree? Well, Oprah did.

"I can't believe how grounded you are," I said. "It's so inspiring."

She turned to me.

"Mastin," she said in her big Oprah voice, motioning all around her, "you don't get all *this* without being grounded."

Oprah has truly figured it out—how to have success and happiness. She isn't defined by what she has; she is firmly rooted in being present and service-minded. With all that Oprah has, she still cared for this little tree. She still notices things that are subtle. It was a major lesson for me. I was amazed at how much detail she paid to little things. For most of my life I hadn't spent much time caring about little things—and I certainly wouldn't have noticed the dying tree. I took it as a reminder to continue to choose contribution over significance.

As our time together wrapped up, Oprah put her arm around Jenna's shoulder and pointed to a window.

"You see that window over there?" she asked. "That's my bedroom. I put your flowers there and will think of you every day." This person, who has a flower garden that would make the queen of Wonderland green with envy, had put *our* flowers in her bedroom window. This was another confirmation that it's all in the details. It's in having the humble graciousness to make us feel seen and Loved.

What a gift to be in her presence, witnessing this magic. I had never seen it demonstrated so clearly before. Humility, openness, and a total ability to see you as you are without judgment—only Love. I will always be grateful that I got to feel that kind of Love personified. To me, Oprah truly embodies the principle of putting contribution to the world as your number one priority.

A few months later I was invited to appear on Oprah's Emmy Award–winning weekly show *Super Soul Sunday*. They wanted to do a feature on the younger generation of spiritual thinkers. I was already on their radar and they asked me who else would be good for the show. I recommended my friends Gabrielle Bernstein and Marie Forleo and it was a done deal. It was one of the most terrifying and fulfilling experiences of my life. It still seems surreal to me.

When I first heard I'd been invited, it didn't feel real. When I was a manager in the music biz, I'd learned a bit about how the TV world works. Things happen so fast that it's really easy to get canceled at the last minute. So I decided it was all a dream. It wasn't until I was at the LA airport flying to Chicago that it hit me: this was really happening! I was so scared I almost didn't get on the plane. Thank God Gabby Bernstein was at the airport with me. Without her, I would probably have stayed in LA. I was so freaked out.

That night Gabby, Marie, and I did some meditation and Kundalini yoga in our hotel. It helped to calm my nerves, but I was still terrified. I barely slept that night. When we got to Harpo the next day, we went into makeup and were suddenly surrounded by producers, assistants, and all the people that make *Super Soul Sunday* happen. Each passing moment I kept feeling like I was going to die. I decided I had nothing good to say and that it would be the worst *Super Soul Sunday* they had ever done.

The set was classic Oprah Winfrey. Gabby, Marie, and I walked onstage. Oprah was already there and the whole audience section was dark. All I could see were the dim silhouettes of people and a faint glare off a camera lens. As we sat down, the cameras started rolling. The first question went to me (dammit!). Oprah asked, "Mastin, can you really be spiritually aware at thirty?" I was so terrified I bumbled the answer! I had no idea what was coming out of my mouth. At the end of my answer, Oprah graciously said "Uh-huh," and moved on to Gabby. At this moment I knew it was all downhill. So I checked out mentally for the rest of the show. I could feel my mouth moving, and I knew I was answering questions, but I was not in my body, so the rest of the taping flew by. I walked off the stage thinking, *This was the worst idea ever and everyone is going to hate it.* But backstage I got hugs from Maya, Morgan, and Harriet Seitler, Harpo's EVP. They loved it! I was in shock. What seemed like a disaster in my mind had been well received by those who mattered.

When the show aired, it ended up being one of the most popular episodes to date.

When I look back I see that all the good fortune in my life came as I began to focus on service to others, rather than significance for myself. People often ask how I met Jenna or how I got on *Super Soul Sunday.* I always say that contribution and service is what did it. There was no real strategy. I did not pitch myself to be on the show, and I didn't go chasing after Jenna. Both were truly the work of Divine Grace.

Tony Robbins says it best: *Power flows to those that serve.*

The more I serve, the more I add value to other people's

lives, the better my own life seems to be. There are massive miracles waiting if we can just open up and help take away the pain of other people.

It starts with letting go of "I want," praying instead that "Thy will be done." For what I now see is that there is no marketing strategy, social media strategy, Rolodex, or bank account that is as big as God's plan for us. And when it comes to Love, you will meet who you are supposed to meet as long as you trust the path and allow yourself to be used—instead of trying to use others for your own gain.

The best thing about all the ups and downs I've had, and all the hard lessons I've learned, is that I get to share what I've discovered with others. What wisdom I've gained has come through my own pain and suffering. Perhaps by sharing what I know with you, right here and now, you'll be spared the pain of learning these particular lessons the hard way.

— chapter 12 —

THE EPIDEMIC
OF SPIRITUAL
ENTERTAINMENT

Massive action is the cure-all.

—TONY ROBBINS

I WROTE THIS BOOK BECAUSE I FELT THAT SHARING MY story might inspire you to know that you are not alone on your path. That someone has been there, in the darkness and the depths, and made it through to the other side. Perhaps I can be a way-shower for you, letting you know that there is indeed hope, there is indeed a way out. I would be well and truly bummed if you read this book and just put it back on the shelf or filed it away on your iPad, and did nothing with the information. In fact, that would be a tragedy to me. My deepest hope is that this book inspires you to take action. Like, a *lot* of action. Tons.

Personal growth without action is what I've come to call *spiritual entertainment*. When I say the word *entertainment*, what comes to mind? Your favorite book or movie? Perhaps a concert, TV show, or sporting event? These all count as entertainments. Entertainment, as I define it, is anything that you passively watch that gives you a temporary emotional experience.

Now, think about your favorite movie for a moment. Why do you love it so much? For most of us, it's because we identify with the hero. Often they are stuck in some way—they're unexpressed and unfulfilled, yearning for something more. Just like *us*. But lucky for them, something happens: a new adventure is offered. The hero is scared, and so are we. Will they dare undertake this adventure . . . or not? Usually they do, and we get to watch them go on the Hero's Journey we learned about back in Chapter 5.

In fact, this is the moment where the Hero's Journey begins. Some circumstance forces the hero onto their adventure. Watching the movie, we're excited that they've come out of their comfort zone. Next up, they meet friends and mentors to show them the way. They are learning, and so are we. Then the tests come. Not everyone is who they say they are; friends and enemies make themselves known. A deeper commitment has to be made to some cause or to our own dream. It's scary to up their game and yet they do it. Watching, we are thrilled. Unfortunately the road gets rockier, and eventually all seems lost. The hero may even die—and us along with them. Death seems like such a tragic outcome to the journey. And yet, by some miracle, the hero is reborn! We stand in awe of their courage and determination. With a new sense of purpose and clarity that fear is the only enemy, the hero finally really ups their game—arriving victorious at the end of their adventure. We, too, feel the victory—as if we were on the adventure right there with them.

This is why we love *Star Wars*, *Star Trek*, *Harry Potter*, *The Matrix*, *Eat Pray Love*, *Wild*, *Bridget Jones's Diary*, and so many other stories of heroism, valor, and love. They make us feel all of our emotions over the course of the journey, and we learn about ourselves through the characters.

Yet at the end of the movie, what do we have—really?

We have an emotional catharsis, sure. But at the end of the night, we go home. The next day we wake up as if nothing happened. We go on with our lives. That's because a movie is just entertainment.

What I've started to see is that we can go through the *exact* same experience when we get into personal-growth work. Seriously, think about it. When you read your favorite inspirational book, don't you go on some sort of emotional journey? Reading this very book, haven't there been highs and lows? Did you have moments of inspiration and insight? I've had so many aha moments reading the work of the people that I've mentioned in this book. I would read a paragraph and it would be like a miracle had occurred. It would feel like the clouds parted, the whole Uni-verse came into alignment, and everything—I mean *everything*—suddenly made sense. Past, present, and future, I understood why everything in my life had happened as it did. I got that all beings have the power of choice and that all is in Divine order. It was like I became one with the cosmos and God.

And then I would wake up the next day and think to myself, *What was that thing I just read?* Truth is, many of those aha moments didn't change me. They were but fleeting moments of inspiration, of connection to the Divine.

Don't get me wrong—I am incredibly grateful for those moments. Ultimately they showed me I could feel just as good off drugs as I did on drugs. And yet, in some way, they weren't that different from doing drugs. They were as fleeting as the experience of being high, but without the hangovers.

I started to see this was a pattern in my own life. After doing Date with Destiny, I saw that most of my spiritual work was just spiritual entertainment; I wasn't backing it up with action. I was running from book to book to book, seminar to seminar, and one life coach or therapist to another—always chasing the spiritual high. While I credit Kundalini yoga for much of my success today, I see that at times I also used yoga as spiritual entertainment.

I've come to recognize that I can't asana away my pain, I can't green juice away my childhood resentments, and I surely can't gluten-free away my heartbreak. I can try and escape to Bali (where I happen to be writing this book), but no matter where I go, I bring myself and my issues with me.

It's not until we have the courage to truly feel our feelings— honestly and without self-judgment (or at least, as little self-judgment as possible)—that we begin to heal. But even *that's* not enough. Salvation comes only if we take action. You can understand something without truly *knowing* it. If you want to see what you truly know, look at your actions. *What you are doing is what you know.* Everything else is just an understanding that you haven't put into practice yet.

I've struggled with weight all my life. As of the writing of this book, I *understand* how to lose weight, but I don't *know how to* lose weight. From the time I finish this book to when it comes out, my intention is to *know how to* lose weight—to take massive action toward reaching a goal I've had for a long time. I want it to actually inspire you to *do something*, too.

As a first step, let's take a pledge together. I call this the Spiritual Entertainment Pledge. Place your left hand over your heart. Raise your right hand and say the following out loud:

I promise, on my honor
From this day forward
To no longer participate in spiritual entertainment
I am a person of action
I will live the questions
But not wait for answers to take action
I trust my intuition
I trust the Divine to always catch me
Uncertainty is my friend
And each day I surrender my will to Divine Will
I am a person of massive action
Fear is a compass showing me where to go
I use fear as fuel
And will take action until I reach the outcome I want
So help me (insert whatever name you call the Divine).

Now, give yourself a pat on the back. As Obi-Wan said to Luke, *"You have taken your first step into a larger world."*

Then the question becomes, *What do I do next?*

Here is a tip I've learned along the way. It has helped me begin to step out of the spiritual entertainment bubble and into the embodiment of virtue. Remember that even though you are on a transformational journey, and even though you are trying to create change, *you are not trying to change or fix yourself.*

How does the idea of "fixing" yourself *feel*? Honestly, how does it feel? Think about it. *Fixing* yourself. Do you need to be *fixed*? To me, that feels like a heavy and impossible task. I think of being a human as kind of like owning a house. Anyone who's ever owned a house knows that you are never "done." You are the steward of a long-term project that is never complete. Once one thing breaks and you fix it, then another thing breaks. Then another and another. Even if something hasn't broken in a while, you'll have property taxes due. Once those are paid, something will break again. The house is never "fixed"—it's never complete. It's an ongoing project until you either sell or die.

The same is true for personal development. You are a long-term project that is constantly growing, changing, learning, and expanding. (You can't even put yourself on the market when you're sick of yourself!) So personal growth is not about fixing yourself; it's about *changing your patterns*.

To me, changing your patterns feels much better—and it's actually doable. The question to ask is, *What patterns do you want to change and why?* The answers reveal a lot more about who you really are. You—in all your imperfect, unfixable vulnerability. We are not here to "get it right."

We're here to try, learn, and try again—wiser and stronger each time.

why all the razzle-dazzle of spiritual entertainment?

So why is it so easy to fall into the trap of spiritual entertainment? There are several reasons. First among them is that as much as we want to change, we are also terrified of uncertainty. We'd almost rather stick to our old patterns than risk doing something different. That's why it's so easy to get lost in the world of self-help books, seminars, yoga, and therapy. We *feel* like we are making progress, but in truth we may actually be spinning our wheels and not taking any action. I believe in self-help. I practice yoga and I attend lots of seminars. But thankfully I've learned to add *action toward fear and uncertainty* into my practice. That's the missing ingredient in so many seekers' paths—the action that follows the *aha!*

Another way we avoid uncertainty is to get overly caught up in the story of our past—what happened to us and when. At the end of 5, 10, or 15 years of seeking we'll have a whole book filled with what happened. Yet we aren't asking, *What do I want to create and why? How can I serve others with this creation?* Because those questions—which create *forward* momentum—take us into the unknown.

Another reason we get lost in spiritual entertainment is that a whole generation of spiritual seekers has bought into a giant lie about our spiritual path. That lie is this:

Fear is the opposite of Love.

No single belief has spawned more spiritual entertainment than this one. Why? Because we actually believe it to be literally true, in all cases. When we believe that Love is the opposite of fear, we tend to make ourselves wrong for being afraid. But the only way for us to truly be happy is to give and to grow. And if we are going to grow, we will always be facing uncertainty—which is, by its very nature, scary.

You see, fear is not the opposite of Love. Fear is a biological and biochemical response to uncertainty.

Think about it. Is it unLoving to be afraid of an attacker? Is it unLoving to fear for the safety of your child? Is it unLoving to be scared of uncertainty in any way?

Our biological design would say no. Whenever there is uncertainty in our lives, our biology kicks in. A part of our brain called the amygdala fires off the fight-or-flight response—aka fear. (In women it can also be the mend-and-attend response—if I can't kill it or run from it, maybe I'll survive if I take care of it.) All kinds of hormones get triggered, including cortisol and adrenaline, and our digestion slows down and can even turn off. The body is prepping to fight or to flee, so it sends all of our blood to our hands and feet.

And the result in modern-day times? Stressed-out overachievers who have adrenal fatigue or just feel burned out, with tense and inflexible bodies that can't seem to take a crap or digest anything.

In other words, the amygdala generates the fear response. So if fear were the opposite of Love, then why would our

Loving Creator give us an amygdala? Is it a mistake? I don't think so. The amygdala has a very kind and benevolent purpose. No big deal—just our *survival!* If we didn't feel afraid, we wouldn't be able to evolve and grow and survive. Fear allows us to be discerning and make better choices. It's an evolutionary advantage that we have an amygdala and can feel fear. You and I both want to be alive! And we have our amygdalas to thank for the fact that we are. Fear is not the opposite of Love; fear is a biological response to uncertainty designed for our own protection. Yet the message we modern-day seekers get is that our own self-preserving biology is killing our dreams.

This belief causes two major blocks to living beyond spiritual entertainment. First, *it causes us to make ourselves wrong for being afraid.* As Tony Robbins so wisely once told me, "Use fear as fuel." (One exception is if you are actually in mortal danger. Don't go toward the guy in the alley who's pointing a gun in your direction, okay?)

I get so mad when I see spiritual leaders try to convince their tribe to "live a fearless life." As I said earlier, if you want to live a fearless life, my friend, you'll have to stay in your comfort zone. The only way to be truly happy is to be growing. And the thing you must do to grow is face uncertainty. Uncertainty comes with fear in tow. The two are nearly inseparable.

The second way the belief that "fear is the opposite of Love" blocks our spiritual journey is that it has us make ourselves wrong for having negative thoughts. The negative mind has its place. In the Kundalini tradition, there are three aspects to the mind: the positive mind, the neutral mind, and the negative mind.

The negative mind is associated with discernment, applying the lessons we learned in the past. We *need* negativity; it literally saves us from making the same old mistakes. When we believe that we must release all negative thoughts we block off a huge part of our inner wisdom—and we make it almost impossible to actually move forward.

Quite the opposite of being the enemy, fear is a *compass*. It shows you where to go. For example, I was never more scared than when I appeared on *Super Soul Sunday*. I was equally terrified the first time I spoke on a Hay House stage in front of a few thousand people. I was terrified before my first retreats in Maui and Bali, and before I kissed Jenna the first time.

Of course I felt fear—in each of these cases I knew, on some level, that my life was about to change. But I didn't know how. I was uncertain.

Fear is the necessary precursor to change. We must become comfortable with our fear. Everything we want and need can be found in the unknown territory of fear and uncertainty.

If I could help you change only one pattern, it would be your relationship with uncertainty. Uncertainty is inevitable in life. It's also *impersonal*.

What do I mean by "impersonal"? Think about gravity for a moment. Gravity is a force that affects every area of your life—your posture, your digestion, your business, your health and well-being. It impacts the economy, your travel, your home—literally everything in your life. Yet gravity is entirely impersonal. It doesn't care how you relate to it. It will operate like gravity regardless of whether you like it or not.

If you went to the tallest building in New York City and jumped off without a parachute, what would happen? You guessed it—splat. You're dead. Would you die because gravity hates you? Would you die because gravity thought you deserved it? Would you die because that's what gravity does to people like you?

Of course not. You would die because you had *an unhealthy relationship to gravity*. This is just how gravity operates. If you changed just one pattern of behavior, the outcome would be totally different. I'm not talking about making more money, losing weight, or healing your relationship with your parents. To avoid being annihilated by gravity you wouldn't need to read a single self-help book.

All you'd need to do would be to put on a parachute.

A simple move, but one that has a dramatically different outcome—the difference, literally, between life and death. Well, the same holds true when it comes to our relationship to uncertainty. We've gotten it all backward. We don't realize that uncertainty is a force that will always be there, in every area of our lives, whether we want it or not. The question we need to ask is not how to get rid of uncertainty, but how to change our patterns so we're relating to it well.

Tony Robbins always says *"The quality of your life is the quality of your relationship to uncertainty."*

In my work with hundreds of one-on-one clients, and tens of thousands of clients online and in our sold-out retreats and workshops all over the world, I've discovered that Tony is right. When our clients focus on changing their relationship to uncertainty, everything in their life changes, too.

Why? Well, like gravity, uncertainty affects every single area of your life. You have uncertainty in your finances, your family relationships, your health, your business, and your romantic partnerships (or lack thereof). If we get really honest with ourselves, there is uncertainty everywhere we look. And it is our relationship to this uncertainty that will affect the outcome of our lives.

I've seen addicts progress by leaps and bounds when they see that uncertainty is the trigger for their addiction. I've seen entrepreneurs get unstuck and double their sales when they've realized that a fear of uncertainty was causing them to play small. I've seen couples come back to Love—or break up—once they understand how uncertainty has been driving them behind the scenes.

We are caught up in spiritual entertainment because at our core we are terrified of the uncertainty all the spiritual work brings. Trusting the Divine is scary business. It might sound good, but even *Jesus* had a hard time doing it. And look what happened to him? It got him killed (though he did come back to life). But in truth, there is a part of us that *must* die if we are to live spiritual, thriving lives. We must begin to put our survival instincts on the back burner and take a leap of faith into the arms of God. I'm not saying to go and make a bunch of foolish decisions, but generally speaking we are not risking as much as we could. As a result we feel stuck, blocked, and less fulfilled.

It's time for our generation of seekers to get real about the spiritual entertainment epidemic. It's time for all of us to quit hiding behind the idea that fear is the opposite of

Love, and instead act in *spite* of fear. With courage. Fear, like everything in the Uni-verse, has a purpose. It is we who have made that purpose wrong, because to see fear any other way would require a massive shift in our lives.

My question for you, dear seeker, is this: *What do you do when you get uncertain?*

you are so much more than you think you are

It's also worth making sure you haven't turned the circumstances of your life into your identity. For example, someone who doesn't have a lot of money in their bank account might say, "I'm poor"—which leaves them feeling powerless and hopeless. But people who are savvy with money might use a different phrase to describe the situation. They might say, "I don't have access to liquid capital at the moment." Same communication ("I have zero cash") but a very different feeling in the body. The latter phrase feels temporary, fixable, and has more hope in it.

What you've decided about yourself and what's possible for you may not have anything to do with *who you really are.* They've just been your circumstances for so long, you mistake them for your identity.

Maybe you think you aren't enough.

That things will never change.

That people like you don't get to live your dreams.

Or that you will never be loveable.

While those might be accurate descriptions of how you feel in the moment, they are not accurate descriptions of *who you really are and what's possible for you.*

This brings me to what I think of as the deepest truth I've discovered over the course of my Hero's Journey thus far.

It goes back to the Sanskrit term *satcitananda* from the Hindu tradition. If you remember, the three root words are used to describe the peak experience of human existence. We've already talked about *ananda*—it means bliss. But, if you dig deeper into *ananda* you discover something else. It also means *bliss is who you are.*

We live in a world filled with so much pain and suffering. How can bliss be who we are? And yet it's true. Below the fear of uncertainty, which operates at the level of your body, there is an infinite Soul—a spirit connected to All That Is. The goal in life is to be in such rapport with your body that your Soul can shine through effortlessly.

And my friend, your Soul doesn't need personal growth. It doesn't need green juice or yoga. That's for your *body*. Once we accept our humanness, the Soul *naturally* shines through. Our humanness needs personal growth, a stronger digestive tract, to be carrying less weight, or a calmer nervous system. All personal growth is for our human side. The Soul is doing just fine.

Accepting our humanness means feeling the feelings we don't want to feel; it means being terrified and moving forward anyway. Scary as it may be, when we choose what brings us bliss, we are truly living God's will in our lives.

Bliss is God's will? That's a big statement. But roll with me for a moment.

Remember what we said about the apple seed? That if you planted an apple seed, an apple tree would grow? I think we can agree that never in the history of time has one planted a (non-GMO) apple seed and had an orange tree emerge. Why not? The answer is stupidly simple and yet profound at the same time.

A seed is like what it came from.

This is a Uni-versal Truth. The fruit that bore the seed is the same fruit the seed will produce. That's God's will. And it's true for us, too. We came from bliss and so it's God's will that we have bliss in our lives. Bliss is what we are—body, mind, and soul. The seed is like what it came from. If you are bliss that means bliss is where you came from. Following your bliss is literally following Divine will in your life. This is why Joseph Campbell said, *"Bliss is the message of God to yourself."*

When we truly know this, everything changes. To live your bliss is the purpose of your life. And in order to embody that purpose—to align yourself with the hero's thread—you must take action into the unknown every single day.

You are going to *face* the unknown, like it or not. It's up to you whether you want to do it consciously or unconsciously.

Grace came into my life when I realized that I never needed God's forgiveness, I was never out of favor, and it wasn't too late. The Divine doesn't forgive, because it doesn't have to; all it does is Love. Therefore no forgiveness is needed. The only forgiveness that is needed in order for us to move forward is our own. This helps us take steps to change our pattern with uncertainty. When we forgive, we don't make right what happened, but we do set ourselves free. Forgiveness is a selfish action that frees us, and it's the best revenge. Grace is the ever-present possibility for us to change some simple patterns in our lives. It's never too late to change, and when we get this and take action, Grace rushes in to show us that indeed life can be made new.

Divine Favor is right there waiting for you to make a few subtle tweaks. My tweaks took me from significance to contribution, from subtle stabs at Jenna's Love to an acceptance of Love, from drugs to yoga, and from being afraid to write to writing every single day of my life. Each of these transitions represents a simple yet powerful pattern I've changed.

I have many more patterns that I need to change, and it's not going to be easy. But I now understand that making these changes is not a question of my worth, my ability, or my enoughness. (The same goes for you, by the way.) Instead, it's a question of becoming aware of the patterns I have that hold me back and then getting about the hard work of creating healthier ones.

We are here to learn. Life celebrates those who try; those who put themselves on the line and take risks, mess up, learn lessons, and try again. When you are willing to risk it all for your bliss—with the trust that something greater than you is guiding your every step—that's when you begin to make the switch from crisis to Grace and begin to live your Hero's Journey. You will never walk alone. If you look deeply, you will see that even in this very moment you are being held. The bad stuff in life isn't a punishment and it will never last.

Because, after all, crisis is a wake-up call. It's often the call to adventure that sparks the Hero's Journey. The only question is—are you going to answer?

MY GREAT PROMISE TO YOU

There is a whisper within you that is dying to be heard. It reminds you of all that you could be, all that you know you already are. The whisper promises Love, dreams fulfilled, and challenges met. Your whisper is a call to new beginnings, great adventures, and to live a life of no regrets. It is subtle and cannot be heard by anyone else. Your tribe can't hear it; they will tell you it is too dangerous and must be ignored. It is your choice what you want to believe; the subtle, unknown Truth within you, or the seemingly secure collective illusion of your Tribe. Your whisper is the Origin of all Creation speaking through you; trusting your whisper is your unique and courageous gift to our World. It is my Great Promise to you that all of existence will conspire to assist you to bring forth your special gift only once you have fully committed to listening to what is heard by you alone.

DAILY LOVE
RESOURCE GUIDE

I DID NOT GET TO WHERE I AM TODAY ALL BY MYSELF. I HAVE had mentors and guides, and gone through many personal growth programs. If you are interested in taking your training beyond this book, here are some great resources for you.

Daily Love Mastery – An online eight-week comprehensive mentoring program that was created to be a one-stop shop for your life transformation. Learn more: http://mastery. dailylove.com

Daily Love Retreats – Journey to a far-off land with us. We have many different retreats ranging from relationship, to personal growth, to writing your book. Learn more: http://dailylove.com/retreats

Daily Love LIVE – A powerful multi-day seminar that we do once a year. It's like Miracle-Gro for your life transformation. Learn more: http://live.dailylove.com

Daily Love Tour – If you want to come to a Daily Love event at a city near you, check out: http://dailylove.com/events

Date with Destiny – This is the best personal growth seminar on the planet. It's Tony Robbins's best work and the seminar that changed my life forever. I think everyone should go to Date with Destiny at least once in their life. Take the plunge! Learn more: http://www.tonyrobbins.com/events

B-School – Marie Forleo's signature program to learn how to make money and a difference online. Learning from Marie was a game changer for me. Learn more: http://bschool.dailylove.com

Dr. Amen SPECT Scan – All of life is experienced in our brains. When you get your brain biochemistry right, everything changes. I highly recommend getting your brain scanned by Dr. Amen; it will be invaluable on your personal growth journey. Learn more: http://www.AmenClinics.com

Kundalini Yoga – This practice changed my life. Daily Love was created in a Kundalini Yoga Center called Golden Bridge in Hollywood, CA. To get some Kundalini Yoga in your life, please visit: http://GBGlobalVillage.com

Sat Siri –My favorite Kundalini Yoga teacher. Please visit: http://www.SatSiriYoga.com

Recovery 2.0 – If you are struggling with addiction or know someone who is, Recovery 2.0 can be a game changer. It's an awesome free conference: http://recovery2point0.com/

Books and CDs that changed my life:

The Power of Myth by Joseph Campbell
The Power of Intention by Wayne Dyer
Inspiration: Your Ultimate Calling by Wayne Dyer
The Power of Now by Eckhart Tolle
A New Earth by Eckhart Tolle
Awaken the Giant Within by Tony Robbins
The Sermon on the Mount by Emmet Fox
Sacred Contracts by Caroline Myss
Anatomy of the Spirit by Caroline Myss
Spiritual Power, Spiritual Practice by Caroline Myss
Energy Anatomy by Caroline Myss
Advanced Energy Anatomy by Caroline Myss
Power vs. Force by Dr. David Hawkins
The Road Less Traveled by M. Scott Peck
The Way of the Superior Man by David Deida
Getting to "I Do" by Pat Allen
Start with Why by Simon Sinek
What Jesus said in Matthew, Mark, Luke and John
Think and Grow Rich by Napoleon Hill
Daring Greatly by Brené Brown
The Big Leap by Gay Hendricks
The Millionaire Messenger by Brendon Burchard
The pH Miracle by Dr. Robert Young
The Body Ecology Diet by Donna Gates
Crazy Sexy Diet by Kris Carr
Clean Eats by Dr. Alejandro Junger
Change Your Brain, Change Your Life by Dr. Daniel Amen
Recovery 2.0 by Tommy Rosen

ACKNOWLEDGMENTS

SELF-MADE PEOPLE DON'T EXIST. ANYONE WHO HAS enjoyed success in the life is able to do so because they have been helped by others. And I can tell you that when it comes to the massive turnaround that my life has taken, it has not been a solo journey.

It's taken a village to help me turn my life around, and the Daily Love is not my doing, but yours. The community is what lifted me out of darkness. It has been my friends, my family, and you—my Daily Lover—who have helped me to recover from the depths of despair.

Never in a million years would I have imagined that I'd be living the life that I am now. I feel blessed. I am grateful. And I owe it all to you.

There are some people who I would like to thank, for their direct impact on my life, and without whom this book and the Daily Love would not exist.

First, my love—Jenna. I write the Daily Love, but you are the Daily Love. I have been so blessed to have you in my life, to be able to call you my person. You show me, every day, what love really is. You are my soul mate, my partner in crime, and my best friend. Thank you for always being there for me.

I have a whole chapter dedicated to the impact my parents have had on my life. Liz and Larry Kipp—thank you for raising me to think critically, to always form my own thoughts about life, and for demonstrating true love and caring. I am my mother's and father's son. You have always been there for me and I am forever grateful.

Tim Lawrence—my best friend. I know that you used to think that getting me into the music business was a massive mistake, but it turned out great—didn't it? You are my best friend till the end. I love you, my brother.

To Dolly and Alan Hall—you have become my family. You did an amazing job raising Jenna, Brooke, Wes, and Amber—it is a gift to be in your lives and for you to be in mine.

Sat Siri—thank you for being my steadfast mate. For allowing me to crash all your Kundalini Yoga classes when I needed them most. For being patient with me. For loving me. And for being true blue. You are my dear friend. I am so excited for you and your new family. It's going to be so exciting to watch Prem grow up into an amazing woman.

To Chris Redlitz and Beverly Parenti. Thank you for being there for me from the beginning. Thank you for believing in me. Thank you for being my friends, my mentors, and helping me find my way. You believed in me when I was in the pool house. For that I am forever grateful.

To Sam Angus, you are an amazing attorney. Thank you for taking a risk on me. You have no idea how much your belief in me gave me confidence when I needed it most.

To Trinka—thank you for always showing me the truth. Reminding me of what's real and helping me recover from the darkest of nights. You are a true friend, a mentor, and someone who has shifted the entire direction of my life. You are so special to me.

To Peter Katsis, you were my first mentor. Your guidance, your passion for your work, and your work ethic still inspires me every day. You move mountains and showed me how to do it. Your clients are lucky to have you as their manager and I was lucky to be your assistant.

Fred Durst—you inspired me to leave Kansas and try to make it in the big city of LA. Thank you for taking a risk on me and hiring me to run Flawless. Even though it only lasted a couple months, you have no idea how much that time in my life meant to me. I will always be a fan and your friend.

To Ofer—thank you for helping me get sober and for being there when I needed you. I know things didn't work out the way that we wanted them to, but I know that they worked out for our greatest and highest good. You were a great teacher for me, you started me on the path to loving myself, and for that I am grateful. You are always in my heart, I love you my friend.

To David Moses—the brief time that I knew you impacted me deeply. You were an amazing aba and your life meant so much to me. Your life truly was your message, and in death you were perhaps the greatest teacher I ever had. You gave me the courage to face my deepest fears and know that I have a precious amount of limited time on this earth. Thank you for this gift. I will never forget the jewel that you've given me.

Jeff Antebi—thank you for showing me how to know my worth. The way that you managed Gnarls Barkley stays with me to this day.

John Boyle—you and MB took a risk on me. Thank you for that. And thank you for showing me the ropes in the clothing business. Thank you for taking a risk on Emma Burgess with me. You are a true friend.

Michael Lippman—buddy, thank you for helping me discover that I love screenwriting and telling stories. I often think about our writing time together and treasure those memories to this day.

To Lolita, Yvonne, and Daneille. Thank you for allowing me to stay in your pool house. You will always be family to me. Thank you for being there when I needed you most.

To Agapi Stassinopoulos and Arianna Huffington. Thank you for your charity and for helping me in the darkest of nights. Agapi—we'll always have "Hay House" and our manifesting dance. You guys walk your talk and I am so grateful to call you my friends.

Tommy Rosen and Kia Miller. I love you guys so much. Your couch was a saving grace. Thank you for taking me in and believing in me. Thank you for reintroducing me to yoga, alkaline living, and green juice. I'll never forget your charity or your love.

Jan Shepherd. Thank you for being one of my LA moms. Thank you for teaching me it is all about grounding my dreams and bringing them into the real world. Thank you for letting me crash at your apartment while you were in London. Thank you for loaning me money to get out of that awful deal and for believing in me! I paid you back fast. You are a true friend.

To Sophie Chiche and Leah. You guys brought me back to my heart. I will never forget our time together. Thank you for the "Welcome home" sign. You have no idea how much that has stuck with me to this day. Thank you for all the coconut popcorn nights and for letting me stay with you for almost a year. I wouldn't be here without your love and support. You are family forever.

Ryland Engelhart—thank you for being love, my brother. Thank you for bringing me into your house and giving me a safe place to get grounded again. Thank you for how you show up in the world and who you are being. You are my brother and I love you.

Jason Binn—you changed my life with one phone call. Thank you for believing in me. Thank you for buying me a My.Suit suit. Thank you for introducing me to Tony. You have no idea how much that lunch changed my life. You are a mensch. You are my dear friend. I will forever be grateful.

To Tony and Sage Robbins—I don't know what to say. Meeting you, experiencing your love, your generosity, your compassion, and your heart, was life changing. Thank you for gifting me a ticket to UPW and Date With Destiny. I am committed to paying forward all that I have gained by having you in my life. You are a massive force for good and I am honored to have had the privilege to be impacted by your work.

To Oprah Winfrey. Words cannot describe the impact that you have had on my life. You changed it forever by simply being yourself. I don't know how the forces of life conspired to bring you into my life, but I am grateful they did. Your heart, your intention, and your soul shines through in everything that you do. No one is more deserving of all the success and joy than you. You have inspired a generation to live their best life, including me. Thank you for being the rainbow for us all.

To Joseph Campbell—I never had the privilege to be able to meet you in this lifetime. But I am grateful for your life, your message, your teachings, and your dedication to raising the consciousness of our planet. Your work is now embedded in my DNA. You opened my eyes to a much larger world and your work lives on in the generation of writers, thinkers, and lightworkers that you have inspired through your work. Thank you.

Others I would like to thank: George Lucas, Steven Spielberg, Kathleen Kennedy, JJ Abrams, Alex Kurtzman, Roberto Orci, Lawrence Kasdan, James Cameron, and the Wachowski Brothers—thank you for making films that make me feel nothing but pure "awe."

To Maynard James Keenan—thank you for encouraging me to create something that makes the world a better place. Thank you for Tool. Thank you for A Perfect Circle. Your music touches my soul.

To Katy Perry—girl, thank you for creating anthems of transformation. You are a powerhouse. I hope to meet you one day. Keep roaring!

Thank you to team Daily Love: Anette Sharvit, Jill Esplin, Dylan Schmidt, Natasha Lakos, Peggy Murrah, Angela Spisak, Maria Garcia Crocker, and Jeanette Braddock. Thank you for making everything happen!

Trudy Green—thank you for taking a risk on me. You have become such a stable force in my life. I learn from you every day. Shout out to Ben Rolnick and Danielle Friendman, too!

To my peers: Gabby Bernstein, Kris Carr, Marie Forleo, JJ Virgin, Tim Ferriss, Simon Sinek, Michael Fishman, and Nick Ortner. You guys inspire me to up my game and let me know it's okay to shine.

Special shout-out to Gabby Bernstein—you have become such a dear friend. I am grateful for having you in my life.

To Brendon Burchard—buddy, your work and mission are a game changer. Thank you for all that you offer the world.

To Jeff Walker—you have inspired a generation to LAUNCH including me. Thank you for Product Launch Formula, but most importantly—thank you for how you show up. You are a heart-centered, authentic guy and I am so grateful for your work.

To my amazing Hay House team: Louise Hay, Reid Tracy, Nancy Levin, Richelle Zizian, Margarete Nielsen, Jo Burgess, Jessica Crockett, Ruth Tewkesbury, and Greta Lipp. You guys are amazing. Thank you for bringing me into the Hay House family.

A SPECIAL SHOUT-OUT to Patricia Gift from Hay House—my editor. Without whom this book would have been released two years ago, but you wouldn't be reading it because it would have been terrible. Patty—you make magic with words. Thank you for helping me dig deep.

To Sarah Hall and Danielle Burch and everyone at SHP—thank you for helping me spread Daily Love everywhere.

To my agent—Melissa Flashman at Trident Media Group—thank you for all your help, advice, and strategy. I am looking forward to a career of working together. Please send along my gratitude to Robert Gottlieb.

To Kelly Notaras—OMG. You made this book. You pushed me so hard. You told me when it was crap. You told me when I could up my game. You suffered through Bali illness to help me get this baby done on schedule. You make me a better writer. I can't believe we get to spend every year together creating in Bali. #Awesome

To Pat Verducci—you and I have work to do! I can't wait to write with you in Bali this year. You are such an amazing teacher; your love of story and the craft of screenwriting is infectious. I feel so lucky to have you in my life.

To Holly Perkins—God sent you to me. Thank you for helping me turn my body into my message. You have showed me how to get fit and to get free. You are amazing at what you do.

Adam Cobb—buddy, I can't wait for all that we are going to do together! I want to be just like you. FYCNYC for life! #8DaysAWeek

To my mentors: Caroline Myss, Robert Holden, Wayne Dyer, Eckhart Tolle, Michael Beckwith, David Hawkins, Melodie Beattie, Deepak Chopra, M. Scott Peck, Pia Mellody, David Deida, Alison Armstrong, Arielle Ford, Claire Zammit, Yogi Bhajan, Gurmukh, John Grinder, Richard Bandler, Milton Erickson, Virgina Satir, Frits Perls, and Dr. Daniel Amen—your work has been forever ingrained in my mind. Thank you for your massive contribution to the human race.

A special thanks to Marianne Williamson—you have become a dear friend of mine. Thank you for being the Grace, the miracle, and a massive force of love in my life. You have moved mountains in my life. I will always be here as your #1 fan.

Finally—to the Daily Love community—thank you for allowing me into your lives. You have lifted me up. You have saved me. You have inspired me to keep going. I am here only because of you. Thank you for reading each day. Thank you for retweeting, regramming, quoting and tagging on Facebook. Thank you for coming out to our tour stops, for coming to Daily Love LIVE, to our retreats and commenting on the blog. I am not a self-made man. I am made and reborn because you gave me life again. This book and my life's work are dedicated to you.

With all my love,

Mastin

ABOUT THE AUTHOR

 **Mastin Kipp** is the founder of TheDailyLove.com – a website, daily e-mail and Twitter account that serves soulful inspiration to a new generation. Started as a feed of quotes sent to Mastin's friends, *The Daily Love* shot to fame after a tweet from Kim Kardashian. And a Love monster was born.

Hosting Mastin on her weekly show *Super Soul Sunday*, Oprah dubbed him an 'up-and-coming thought leader of the next generation of spiritual thinkers'. Both an honour and a mouthful.

Mastin's mission is to reconnect people with what makes them happy. Happy people make better choices, and better choices make for a better planet. Mastin completed the 200-hundred-hour YogaWorks teacher training in 2013 and is a certified yoga teacher.

www.thedailylove.com

HAY HOUSE TITLES OF
RELATED INTEREST

YOU CAN HEAL YOUR LIFE, the movie,
starring Louise Hay & Friends
(available as a 1-DVD programme and an expanded 2-DVD set)
Watch the trailer at: www.LouiseHayMovie.com

THE SHIFT, the movie, starring Dr Wayne W. Dyer
(available as a 1-DVD programme and an expanded 2-DVD set)
Watch the trailer at: www.DyerMovie.com

. . .

CHANGE YOUR THOUGHTS, CHANGE YOUR LIFE,
by Dr Wayne W. Dyer

LOVEABILITY: Knowing How to Love and Be Loved,
by Robert Holden PhD

MIRACLES NOW: 108 Life-Changing Tools for Less Stress,
More Flow, and Finding Your True Purpose, by Gabrielle Bernstein

REVEAL: A Sacred Manual for Getting Spiritually Naked,
by Meggan Watterson

All of the above are available at your local bookstore,
or may be ordered by contacting Hay House (see next page).

We hope you enjoyed this Hay House book. If you'd like to receive our online catalogue featuring additional information on Hay House books and products, or if you'd like to find out more about the Hay Foundation, please contact:

Hay House UK, Ltd.,
Astley House, 33 Notting Hill Gate, London W11 3JQ
Phone: 0-20-3675-2450 • *Fax:* 0-20-3675-2451
www.hayhouse.co.uk • www.hayfoundation.org

• • •

Published and distributed in the United States by:
Hay House, Inc., P.O. Box 5100, Carlsbad, CA 92018-5100
Phone: (760) 431-7695 or (800) 654-5126
Fax: (760) 431-6948 or (800) 650-5115
www.hayhouse.com

Published and distributed in Australia by: Hay House Australia Pty. Ltd.,
18/36 Ralph St., Alexandria NSW 2015 • *Phone:* 612-9669-4299 • *Fax:* 612-9669-4144
www.hayhouse.com.au

Published and distributed in the Republic of South Africa by: Hay House SA (Pty),
Ltd., P.O. Box 990, Witkoppen 2068 • *Phone/Fax:* 27-11-467-8904
www.hayhouse.co.za

Published in India by: Hay House Publishers India, Muskaan Complex,
Plot No. 3, B-2, Vasant Kunj, New Delhi 110 070 • *Phone:* 91-11-4176-1620
Fax: 91-11-4176-1630 • www.hayhouse.co.in

Distributed in Canada by: Raincoast Books, 2440 Viking Way, Richmond, B.C. V6V
1N2 • *Phone:* 1-800-663-5714 • *Fax:* 1-800-565-3770 • www.raincoast.com

• • •

Take Your Soul on a Vacation

Visit www.HealYourLife.com® to regroup, recharge, and
reconnect with your own magnificence.
Featuring blogs, mind-body-spirit news, and life-changing
wisdom from Louise Hay and friends.

Visit www.HealYourLife.com today!

Free e-newsletters
FROM HAY HOUSE
THE ULTIMATE RESOURCE FOR INSPIRATION

Be the first to know about Hay House's dollar deals, free downloads, special offers, affirmation cards, giveaways, contests, and more!

- Get exclusive excerpts from our latest releases and videos from **Hay House Present Moments**

- Enjoy uplifting personal stories, how-to articles, and healing advice, along with videos and empowering quotes, within **Heal Your Life**

- Have an inspirational story to tell and a passion for writing? Sharpen your writing skills with insider tips from **Your Writing Life**

*Get inspired, educate yourself,
get a complimentary gift, and share the wisdom!*

SIGN UP NOW
www.HayHouse.com/newsletters.php

HealYourLife.com ♥

HEAL YOUR LIFE ONE THOUGHT AT A TIME . . .

ON LOUISE'S ALL-NEW WEBSITE!

*"Life is bringing me everything
I need and more."*

— Louise Hay

Come to HEALYOURLIFE.COM today and meet the world's best-selling self-help authors; the most popular leading intuitive, health, and success experts; up-and-coming inspirational writers; and new like-minded friends who will share their insights, experiences, personal stories, and wisdom so you can heal your life and the world around you . . . one thought at a time.

Here are just some of the things you'll get at HealYourLife.com:

- DAILY AFFIRMATIONS
- CAPTIVATING VIDEO CLIPS
- EXCLUSIVE BOOK REVIEWS
- AUTHOR BLOGS
- LIVE TWITTER AND FACEBOOK FEEDS
- BEHIND-THE-SCENES SCOOPS
- LIVE STREAMING RADIO
- "MY LIFE" COMMUNITY OF FRIENDS

PLUS:
- FREE Monthly Contests and Polls
- FREE BONUS gifts, discounts, and newsletters

MAKE IT YOUR HOME PAGE TODAY!

HEAL YOUR LIFE®♥
www.HealYourLife.com®